the
Northland
of New Zealand

-an illustrated guide-

the North Island
of New Zealand

~an illustrated guide~

by Diana and Jeremy Pope
Photographed by Martin Barriball

REED METHUEN

First published 1986

REED METHUEN PUBLISHERS LTD
39 Rawene Road, Auckland 10

ISBN 0 474 00232 2

Typeset by Quickset, Christchurch, New Zealand
Printed by Everbest Printing Co. Ltd, Hong Kong

Acknowledgements

This book is the combined product of the labours of more people than can ever be listed on a single page. In particular, the authors were aided by Sue Upton in Wellington, by Jill Tasker and Keith Legg in London, and by a multitude of government departments, national park rangers and information offices.

Martin Barriball, too, was assisted by numerous individuals and institutions during the course of his 18-month photographic assignment around the country, taking the tens of thousands of photographs from which those for this book were selected. The help, co-operation and friendship he received is warmly remembered and greatly appreciated.

All three were the beneficiaries of the energy and enthusiasm of Jane Parkin, Bill Wieben and Graham Wiremu on the staff of the publisher. Their dedication to the project kept all of us going at times when we might well have flagged. Graham also contributed the text on pp. 50-51.

The publishers in turn would like to thank the following people and institutions for their permission to use material as follows: The Alexander Turnbull Library for historical photographs; Nancy M. Adams for her drawings of alpine flowers; Graham Hampton for his photograph of motorcycling on p. 35; Fraser Gardyne for his photograph of Putiki Church on p. 77; the Manawatu Art Gallery for the Colin McCahon painting on p. 79; the New Zealand Co-operative Rennet Company for the photograph of cheese production on p. 75; Mr G.E. Smith of the Pukeiti Rhododendron Trust for the photograph on p. 75, and Rodney Smith for his photograph of glow-worms on p. 42. Thanks are also due to John Ashton, John Drawbridge, Gordon Walters and Downstage Theatre for their assistance with illustrative material.

There were, in addition, a huge number of people who answered queries, checked references and did whatever they could to keep the text as accurate as possible – not to mention the many users of the authors' *Mobil New Zealand Travel guide – North Island* and *Mobil New Zealand Travel Guide – South Island,* who have written to them with helpful suggestions. However, responsibility for the factual content and for the opinions expressed lies solely with the authors.

The forebearance of Adam, Jemima and Samuel Pope is also worthy of record. They have seen more of their country than most, and perhaps more than they might have wished!

Diana and Jeremy Pope

The North Island

Three Kings Is.
Spirits Bay
C. Reinga
North Cape
C. Maria van Diemen
Ninety
Mile
Beach
Doubtless Bay
Ahipara Bay
Kaitaia
Kerikeri
Bay of Islands
C Brett
Kawakawa
Kaikohe
Poor Knights Is.
Hikurangi
Hokianga Harbour
WHANGAREI
Dargaville
Marsden Point
Hen and Chicken Is.
Little Barrier I.
Wellsford
Great Barrier I.
Kaipara Harbour
Warkworth
HAURAKI GULF
Mercury Is.
Helensville
Waiheke I.
COROMANDEL PENINSULA
AUCKLAND
Pukekohe
Thames
Thames
Waikato
Paeroa
Mayor I.
Waihi
BAY
White I.
C Runaway
Te Aroha
Huntly
Morrinsville
Mt. Maunganui
OF
Te Araroa
East Cape
Raglan
TAURANGA
Matamata
Te Puke
PLENTY
Motu
Te Kaha
Ruatoria
HAMILTON
Cambridge
L. Rotorua
Whakatane
Hikurangi
Te Awamutu
Opotiki
Otorohanga
ROTORUA
Kawerau
Tokoroa
Rangitaiki
Tolaga Bay
Te Kuiti
Murupara
Wairakei
NORTH
TARANAKI BIGHT
Taumaranui
L. Taupo
Taupo
L. Waikaremoana
GISBORNE
Waitara
Turangi
KAIMANAWA RA.
NEW PLYMOUTH
Tongariro
Ngauruhoe
Wairoa
Mohaka
RUAPEHU
Mahia Peninsula
Mt Egmont
Stratford
HAWKE BAY
Opunake
Ohakune
Waiouru
NAPIER
Hawera
Taihape
HASTINGS
C Kidnappers
Patea
Havelock North
SOUTH
WANGANUI
Wanganui
Waipukurau
TARANAKI BIGHT
Marton
Feilding
Dannevirke
RUAHINE RA.
Rangitikei
Woodville
PALMERSTON NORTH
Pahiatua
Manawatu
Foxton
Tukituki
Otaki
Levin
Kapiti I.
TARARUAS
Castle Point
Paraparaumu
MASTERTON
Carterton
COOK STRAIT
Featherston
Wairarapa
WELLINGTON
C. Palliser

Contents

Introduction

The North Island of New Zealand – on the south-western perimeter of Polynesia – bears a singularly unimaginative name for an island so crowded with diversity. Stretching about 800km from north to south, it ranges in climate from the sub-tropical "Winterless North" to the markedly more temperate climes of Wellington. Scenically, the landscape embraces farming regions of prodigious productivity, thermal areas with geysers and boiling mud pools, active volcanoes and, to the north, a myriad of islands whose magic is irresistible for those with access to boats. In its wonderfully varied flora and fauna, the Island boasts abundant trout, the mainland gannets of Cape Kidnappers, the magnificent Waipoua Kauri Forest, and plant life that varies markedly in tune with climatic variations. Culturally, too, the North Island is diverse, including as it does not only the overwhelming majority of the indigenous Maori population but also, as a culmination of several decades of immigration, sufficient Polynesian Islanders for Auckland to be the region's unofficial "capital".

New Zealand's two largest cities are also in the North Island – Auckland, the country's metropolis, straddles the Waitemata and Manukau Harbours, and Wellington, the country's capital, rests by its southernmost tip, in the eye of the "roaring forties".

In the heart of the Island lies the expanse of trout-filled Lake Taupo, a vast volcanic crater, with the still active peaks of the Tongariro National Park to the south and, immediately north, the full-throated roar and billowing steam of the geothermal vents of Wairakei, harnessed to provide electric power. Also on the Volcanic Plateau are the thermal wonders of Rotorua, where the colours and contours of silica terracing compete for attention with the splash of geysers and the bubble-and-plop of boiling mud. Rotorua, too, has its lake, alive with the love story of Hinemoa, the Maori maiden who by night escaped from her family and swam to her lover, Tutanekei, on Mokoia Island, guided only by the plaintive music of his nose-flute. Deep in the heart of the King Country (whence the followers of the Maori King took refuge after the wars with the settlers were lost) lie the magic limestone tracery and the glow-worm spangled canopy of the Waitomo Caves.

The Europeans' prosaic names for the principal islands contrast with those of the Maori, to whom the North Island was Te Ika a Maui (the fish of Maui). The configuration of today's maps confirms the early imagery, with the peninsula of Northland unquestionably the fish's tail, the bulges of Taranaki and the East Cape its fins, and the capital city of Wellington resting at its mouth, on the very nostrils of the fish of Maui. The arch of mountains that stretches from Wellington north through much of the Island's central regions, too, is truly a backbone. In some versions of the legend Maui made his huge catch while fishing from the South Island, which itself resembles an upturned canoe.

Nor is the Maui legend without scientific foundation, as the Island, indeed the country, is geologically "young", having emerged from the sea comparatively recently – a fact reflected in its raw and unweathered landscape.

Maui himself – a demi-god in the twilight zone where legend and oral history fuse – appears over much of Polynesia. The North Island, in size the greatest, is by no means his only "fish", giving rise to the belief that Maui was a creator-discoverer who, as he journeyed into the unknown, seemed to "fish" strange islands from beneath the horizon. Subsequent migration from the Society Islands peopled the land. Their double-hulled canoes, which sailed in times when even the most intrepid of European explorers would not dare venture out of sight of land, transported a Polynesian culture across a vast void of ocean. Adapting over time to a very different environment, this was transformed into the distinctive culture of the Maori.

As horticulture became more widely practised, Maori culture flourished most spectacularly in the North Island – where at least some of the plants originating from warmer climes, such as the kumara (sweet potato), could grow – while at the time of the arrival of the first Europeans, the Maori over much of the South Island tended to be the less successful tribes, surviving more as hunter gatherers than as secure horticulturalists.

This disparity between the Islands is still seen today, with the bulk of the Maori population living in the North Island. For the traveller this is reflected in the number and spread of characteristic Maori meeting-houses, both venerable and modern.

The Maori progenitors probably arrived in New Zealand about a thousand years ago; whether by accident or by design will probably never be known. Discovery by Europeans dates from the Dutch explorer, Abel Tasman, in 1642, though after being attacked by South Island Maori he sailed away without even setting foot on the land he had taken to be a part of South America. Captain James Cook, a dour Yorkshireman, followed, in 1769 charting the country more accurately and claiming the North and the South Island – separately – for Britain "by right of discovery". His first landfall, and Young Nick, the cabin boy who first sighted land, are well recorded there.

In the wake of Cook came whalers, sealers, and even the British navy to plunder Northland's and Coromandel's extensive kauri forests for spars for sailing ships. Such was the assault over the years that today the Waipoua Forest, north of Whangarei, is the only substantial and accessible Kauri stand remaining.

The effect of the visitors on the Maori population was no less dramatic. For the traders introduced firearms and the level of inter-tribal warfare, previously sustainable, quickly escalated to near-genocide. Influenza and measles epidemics added further to the toll. In keeping with the times, too, missionaries followed.

Both traders and missionaries established themselves under the protection of the more successful tribes, predominately in the north of the country – the former for access to their produce (in the main, flax); the latter to save their souls. Both are recalled in and around the Bay of Islands – the cradle of New Zealand's recent history – where early mission houses at Kerikeri, Waimate North and Russell, and a number of early churches, remain as testimony to early ecclesiastical endeavour.

It was also on the shores of the Bay of Islands, at Waitangi, where lived James Busby, appointed in 1832 as the first "British Resident" to protect the Maori from rapacious British traders. Finally the excesses of the whalers, traders, and fortune-seekers on the edge of civilisation, together with the pleas of outraged missionaries, drove the British government reluctantly to annex the new land and add it to its Empire – ostensibly with the consent of the chiefs, whose people were dispirited by the twin scourges of disease and war. This was achieved by means of a controversial treaty (so called despite its never having been regarded as such by either Britain or the government of an independent New Zealand). The Treaty of Waitangi, signed on the lawns of Busby's home in 1840, was patently misunderstood by many of the chiefly signatories. Busby's home and grounds are preserved as a continuing reminder of the events which took place there.

It was just across the Bay, at today's Russell, that Hone Heke, the very first chief to have signed the Treaty, became the first to repudiate it – by chopping down the celebrated flagpole (and with it the Union flag), not once but fully four times.

Settlers began pouring in, predominantly from Britain, starting a process that has still not ended. The cities of Auckland (1840), Wellington (1840), Wanganui (1840), New Plymouth (1841) and Nelson (1841) were soon established. War flared. First in Northland, it later engulfed much of the central North Island, where a number of battle sites, and the occasional redoubt and once-fortified church, remain as present-day reminders. In the Bay of Plenty, the only missionary to die at the hands of the Maori fell victim to the Hauhau uprising, a cult whose ceremonies centred on tall niu poles, two of which survive on the Wanganui River, near Taumarunui. The missionary's church, now dedicated to St Stephen the Martyr, remains at Opotiki.

The Wars were essentially over land – Europeans coveting Maori land and, in common with other settler societies, seeing only what they perceived as under-utilisation. They wholly failed to comprehend either the significance of land in Maori tradition and life or the resulting reluctance to sell. Having provoked the conflict, the settlers then used it as a pretext to "punish" the tribes who had resisted the new-comers, and found it appropriate to confiscate their land in acquisitions that over a century later are still a source of frustration and discontent.

Much of today's best farmland – in the Waikato, the Taranaki and the Bay of Plenty – was acquired in this way. In recent years the question of outstanding claims for compensation have come increasingly to the fore, and in 1978, Mount Egmont, the sacred mountain of the Taranaki tribes and repository for the bones of its chiefs, was returned to the tribes to enable them voluntarily – and not as a consequence of confiscation – to donate it to the nation as the centrepiece of a national park.

To consolidate the land gains, a railway (completed in 1908) was constructed through the centre of the North Island, linking Auckland and Wellington. Vast areas were cleared of native forest and, responding to the advent of refrigeration, the country became in effect one large, sea-girthed farm supplying the British market with huge quantities of butter, cheese and lamb. As Britain's "most loyal colony", it also wholeheartedly joined in its European wars.

Britain's entry into the European Economic Community in 1973 has had a traumatic effect on the country's economy, but tangible signs of diversification can be seen, for example among the energy projects of the Taranaki, the kiwifruit vines of the Bay of Plenty, the Glenbrook steel mill (based on local ironsands), the vineyards of Henderson and of Hawkes Bay, and the vast forestry undertakings on and near the volcanic plateau. The movement into industry is reflected in the burgeoning of Auckland. Despite the country's rural roots, about 84 percent of the population now lives in urban areas, and dependence on agricultural exports, though still comparatively high at over 50 percent, is greatly reduced from the 70 percent of only a few years ago.

Today, travelling through the North Island one sees a landscape in part heavily modified, but seldom tamed, a landscape which has witnessed turbulence in all its aspects – geological, historical and ecological.

The far north

ROAD TO REINGA *Much of the area the road dissects has escaped the encroachment of sand only through the efforts of farmer and forester.*

A FABLED POHUTUKAWA Down its roots went the departing spirits.

Fabled in legend and enshrined in the folklore of both Maori and Pakeha, Northland is both a beginning and an end. For the Pakeha it marks the origins of the missionary work that led inexorably to the country's being annexed by Britain; for the Maori it was from Cape Reinga, a point of the peninsula which cleaves the Tasman Sea from the Pacific Ocean, that the spirits of the departed bade farewell to Aotearoa and began a subterranean journey back to their legendary "Hawaiki" homeland.

Yet other compelling claims compete for attention. The climate in the far north is truly sub-tropical, the coastline enticing, the beaches inviting. It is a region in which to linger, in which to move slowly – yet one in which a bumpy bus ride to Cape Reinga along Ninety Mile Beach, complete with racy commentary, can be a highlight. If not completely "winterless", the weather is hospitable at all times of the year and is in summer tempered by the proximity of the sea. Kauri forest once covered much of the region, leaving behind a legacy of precious gum, which was later plundered by hordes of fortune-seeking gum diggers. Many men prospered, but the land, already leached by kauri leaves, suffered grievously. Even today the soil is poor and cultivation sparse; but forestry ventures promise new prosperity and stability for the region.

Aupouri Forest A vast area of hitherto drifting sand dunes along a lengthy expanse of Ninety Mile Beach has been anchored successfully by an afforestation programme designed to preserve farmland but yielding unexpectedly good results in timber. The sand is at first checked by the planting of grasses, which then shelter lupin. In turn the lupin nurtures and feeds pine trees through their infancy.

Cape Reinga Popularly regarded as the country's most northerly point (an honour that in fact belongs to the less accessible Surville Cliffs to the east), Cape Reinga affords a dramatic view of the joinder of Pacific Ocean and Tasman Sea, while its quaint lighthouse awaits its obligatory photograph. Here too is the gnarled pohutukawa of Maori legend. Clinging tenaciously to an alien cliff face, the tree is the departing place for spirits.

CAPE REINGA'S LIGHTHOUSE *The end of the road and a view of where sea and ocean meet.*

HOUSE CARVING *In the Wagener Museum.*

TWO DISTINCTIVE TOWERS The Ratana church at Te Kao reflects the symbolism of a religious sect founded in the 1920s around charismatic Wiremu Ratana, a successful faith-healer from near Wanganui. The teaching is basically Christian, the following largely Maori. The twin towers represent the founder's sons, both saints of the church, named for the Greek letters Alpha and Omega, the beginning and the end.

MAGNETIC MANGONUI *A township on Doubtless Bay, born of the early kauri timber trade.*

WAGENER MUSEUM *Venerable antique gramophones enliven a varied collection of memorabilia at Houhora Heads.*

NINETY MILE BEACH *The bus to Reinga seems lost in the heat of shimmering sand.*

Doubtless Bay A vast crescent of golden shimmering sand and a series of delightful coves draw throngs of holiday-makers here in summer. Cook did not enter the bay when he sailed past here in 1769, but after pondering whether the northern peninsula was an island he concluded, rightly, "Doubtless, a bay"

Houhora Once crowded with fortune-seeking gum diggers, the settlement is but a shadow of its former self. Claims for attention lie in its tavern (the country's most northerly) and, more cogently, in the museum at Houhora

Heads which was founded by descendants of a Pole who came here in the 1850s. The beach is favoured by fishermen, and local tales tell of smugglers. A good place for picnicking and camping.

Te Kao Prominent here are the distinctive towers of the Ratana church (*pictured*).

Kaitaia The main centre of "the north" serves surrounding farmland and prospers visibly from the visitors lured here from the south. Many use the town as a base from which to explore the region. Of special interest is a rumbustious bus ride to Cape Reinga, with one leg following Ninety Mile Beach – a corrosive stretch which most will wish to spare their cars.

Ninety Mile Beach The beach, though lengthy, does not merit its name: it is 90 kilometres rather than 90 miles long. Each summer the scene of a hugely popular and well-rewarded fishing contest, it also witnessed the setting of a world land speed record in 1932 and acted as runway for Kingsford-Smith's epic re-

turn crossing of the Tasman a year later. Today the beach's reputation as a prime source of the treasured toheroa is wearing distinctly thin, as dwindling numbers of the sought-after shellfish have led to extremely limited "seasons" and even at times total bans on their being taken. The related tuatua, though, are found in substantial numbers and are a flavoursome substitute.

Parengarenga Harbour The bar here glistens with silica sand used in glassmaking.

Whangaroa Harbour The harbour stands in contrast to the inlets of the Bay of Islands, and is given unique character by its curious pinnacles, all of which bear biblical names. There is excellent boating here, though sailors might pause to recall the fate of the *Boyd*, whose passengers and crew almost all fell victim to a surprise attack here in 1809 by a local tribe. The "Boyd Massacre" was widely publicised and for a time deterred other would-be visitors. Today the harbour is a vision of tranquillity.

CAMPING Camp sites are not as plentiful as might be thought in the extreme north, but appealing sites are at Houhora and at Taputupoto Bay – the country's northernmost camping ground (*above*). Cape Reinga itself, though used to visitors, has no facilities and prospective campers can be taken by surprise.

CAPE MARIA VAN DIEMEN *Of the place-names bestowed by Abel Tasman in 1642, only two have survived: the others were supplanted by Cook or have reverted to their original Maori names. The cape (or more correctly an islet of it) was the last part of the country seen by Tasman, and is named for the wife of his sponsor, the Governor of the Dutch East India Company in Batavia. The other surviving name is that of the Three Kings Islands, offshore from Reinga, where Tasman spent Epiphany.*

WHANGAROA ON HORSEBACK *One way to attain a harbour view.*

PINNACLES *Uneven erosion of hard and soft rock has created a sharply defined landscape near Whangaroa.*

The Bay of Islands

MORNING OVER THE BAY OF ISLANDS *It has long forsaken its bawdy image of 150 years ago, with the bustle of yachts and holidaymakers replacing the hustle of licentious whalers.*

"The cradle of New Zealand's history" holds endless fascination, whatever one's inclination. Here ride the shadows of such giants of the past as Cook, Charles Darwin, the mighty Hongi Hika and his nephew, Hone Heke. Here, too, dawned both Christianity and British rule, tangible reminders of which remain in mission churches and houses, and the venerable Treaty House. A sheltered sea and, especially, big-game fishing are added attractions in a region still largely unspoiled by its popularity.

HIBISCUS FLOWER *Lush vegetation lends a splash of tropical splendour to the north.*

CRUISE SHIP CALLS *Ocean liners mingle with the ever-present yachts and launches.*

RUSSELL'S MUSEUM A working model of Cook's *Endeavour* is one of many exhibits in the Memorial Museum named for the explorer.

AFTER A RECORD-BREAKER *Numerous world-record catches of marlin, tuna, yellowtail, thresher, mako and hammerhead sharks have been taken from local deep-sea fishing launches.*

Bay of Islands There are about 150 islands scattered over the sheltered waters of the Bay, while seaward-probing arms only add to the richness of the seascape. A favourable climate and rich soils lend themselves to intensive farming, and in pre-European times the tribe centred here, the powerful Ngapuhi, came to dominate much of the North Island. The Ngapuhi's affluence attracted traders, whalers and adventurers before New Zealand's first missionary, Samuel Marsden, arrived in 1814 to bring Christianity to a people grown war-weary. A distinctive cross in Rangihoua Bay marks the scene of his first service. Less known, however, is the place on Moturua Island where, in 1772, the French explorer Marion du Fresne buried a bottle containing his claim to the country for France. Along with about 25 of his crew, he was killed shortly afterwards, at Assassination Cove, perhaps for having trespassed on *tapu* (sacred) ground. The Bay is best seen by joining the half-day "cream trip" at Russell or Paihia.

Kaikohe Set on level farmland in the very heart of Northland, the town supports a number of light industries. From the crest of Kaikohe Hill the coastline on both sides of the Island can be seen. Curiously, Kaikohe's memorial to Hone Heke is not to the celebrated chief but to his great-nephew, who died at the age of 40 having still spent almost half his life as a Maori Member of Parliament.

Kawakawa The administrative centre of Bay of Islands County. The Waiomio Caves and the fortified pa site of Ruapekapeka, where Hone Heke's resistance came to an end, are both nearby. In summer an excursion train steams its way to Opua.

Kerikeri Among the most fertile areas in a country renowned for productivity, Kerikeri engenders more than prolific quantities of citrus and sebtropical fruits. Over the years it has also developed a strong tradition for handicrafts, and cottage industries abound. At Kerikeri Inlet a gracious old mission house stands alongside a quaint stone store, which has been restored to its original design by the Historic Places Trust. There, too, a reconstructed Maori village faces across the water to the wooded site of a pa used by Hongi Hika (*c.* 1780–1828), a Ngapuhi chief who ranged over the North Island and as far south as Cook Strait.

STONE STORE, KERIKERI *One of New Zealand's oldest buildings (1833).*

RELICS OF THE DEEP *Kelly Tarlton's Museum of Shipwrecks is unique for the richness of its collections and its shipboard atmosphere.*

LOCAL CRAFTS *Dolphins and marlin fashioned from kauri are some of the craft items available in the area.*

CITRUS FRUIT *Kerikeri orchards are famous for producing huge quantities.*

CREAM TRIP *A celebrated launch run around the Bay with supplies and visitors.*

PACIFIC ROCK OYSTERS *Found only in the upper-tidal rocky zone of northernmost New Zealand, the oysters are farmed commercially and with increasing success. All beds are State owned.*

Ngawha Springs If uninviting in colour, the mercury soda springs are said to have curative properties and to have been used by the Maori for treating wounds received in battle.

Ohaeawai and Lake Omapere Major engagements took place here in 1845 after Hone Heke had sacked Russell and forced the British to evacuate what had been planned as the new colony's capital.

The Redcoats suffered serious casualties, particularly on the second occasion when Heke's men put the British to flight. Thereafter, the Ngapuhi chief's *mana* knew no bounds, though six months later the war in the north was to end in a decisive engagement at Ruapekapeka. The first encounter was by the shores of Lake Omapere, which is less than three metres deep at its maximum point. The Ohaeawai site is now marked by a church.

Opua Although Paihia and Russell are but a short distance apart, the journey by car would be considerable were it not for the Opua ferry.

Paihia Tradition has it that a pioneer missionary, looking for a site for his mission, saw the bay here and exclaimed to his Maori guide: "Pai (good) here!" Fortunately his knowledge of the language was to improve to the point where he could help compile the first Maori dictionary (still a standard text), but the town's name is, in Maori, meaningless – even if its site on the water's edge could not be bettered.

Paihia's early history is also the country's. Here the first ground was con-

secrated and the first church erected; from the beach missionaries launched the first boat. Here, too, the first volume printing was undertaken (by the missionary Colenso who, for the first time, produced the New Testament in the Maori language). The missionary settlement has evolved into a substantial holiday and retirement centre, with an inevitable string of motels and restaurants along the foreshore. Neighbouring Waitangi is only a stone's throw away, but accommodation there is limited, so many who come to visit the Treaty House and who stay overnight do so at Paihia.

At Waitangi Bridge is the fascinating shipboard museum wherein are displayed a variety of objects recovered from some of the most famous of the wrecks around the New Zealand coastline. Treasures include gold, silver, bronze and precious stones, the *Elingamite* treasure and Rothschilds' jewellery.

From the wharf a passenger ferry runs across to Russell, and one can join either the round-the-bays "cream trip" or the boat trip to Cape Brett which passes through a remarkable natural rock tunnel in Piercy Island.

AT ANCHOR *Keelers at Kerikeri Inlet.*

RECONSTRUCTED MAORI VILLAGE *A reconstruction of a pre-European Maori* kainga *(unfortified village) at Kerikeri.*

Waitangi Known as the nation's birthplace, it was here in 1840 that a treaty, purporting to vest sovereignty over the country in Queen Victoria, was signed by the British and a number of local chiefs. Intended as a benign, paternalistic gesture – local Maori were frequently the object of scandalous treatment by visiting British seafarers – it soon turned to tragedy. A local chief, Hone Heke, rebelled against the imposition of the customs duties that followed annexation – taxes that deterred whaling ships from calling and so drastically reduced local trade. This forced the abandonment of Kororareka (Russell) and led to the war in the north. The fighting quelled, war later flared farther south, initially in the Taranaki, when the Government rigidly and illegally enforced fraudulent land sales it had negotiated. The treaty that was to have protected the Maori was thus seen as having denuded them of much of their land. Understandably, the national celebrations which take place on the lawn of the Treaty House on 6 February (*left and right*) and traditionally attended by the Governor-General are viewed by a body of Maori opinion as an annual reminder of a treaty both misrepresented to, and misunderstood by, those who signed it.

The Treaty House itself (*above left*) dates from 1833. It was assembled here from timber pre-cut in Sydney, and served as the home for the first British Resident, James Busby, who helped "negotiate" the treaty that was signed in his garden. In the grounds is an unusual Maori meeting house (*above right*). Usually a *whare runanga* reflects the ancestry and history of a particular tribe, but this, as a memorial to the centenary of the signing of the treaty, incorporates carvings from tribes throughout the country. The house displays an intriguing collection of historical material but not the treaty – that is in the National Archives in Wellington.

KOROMIKO *A native species of* Hebe.

OPUA FERRY *Between Russell and Paihia.*

Russell Russell's waterfront bestows considerable character: trees and Victorian architecture soften a scene marked by the movement of launches and yachts. The annual "tall ships race" (first week of January) contested by ships – ancient and modern – is followed by a hangi (traditional Maori feast) at the boat club. In the village solid Christ Church (1836) bears the scars of past fighting. The only other building to have completely survived the 1845 sacking of the town is the elegant Catholic mission station, Pompallier House. Like the church, however, it too has been radically renovated.

The Bay of Islands is one of the world's top big-game fishing areas and Russell is

geared to cater for fishermen and fishing vessels alike. The season extends from about November to June, although yellowhead can be caught on light tackle between July and September. Launches are available for charter for deep-sea fishing, line fishing, picnic cruises and skin diving. At the wharf one may also join the "cream trip" or other outings to the open sea and Piercy Island.

Waimate North The handsome mission house here was built in 1831 and was the scene of the country's first major farming experiment. The building, the sole survivor of three similar houses built by the missionaries in the 1830s, is open to the public. Set in mag-

WAIMATE MISSION HOUSE *Once a thriving mission farm, later a theological centre.*

nificent grounds, it has been furnished and restored as closely as possible to its original style, thanks largely to records left by its original inhabitants. Many of the early missionaries' possessions are also on display. Built largely of kauri, it has an attractive symmetrical appearance; unusual, however, was the inclusion of the kitchen inside the house rather than in an outhouse as was customary. In the churchyard, noted for some high carved Maori headboards, lie soldiers killed in the war of 1845. Nearby is Bedgood smithy and wheelwright's shop, one of the country's first "industrial complexes".

Whangarei and environs

WHANGAREI FALLS *A pleasant picnic spot.*

THE COLOURS OF THE NORTH *Typical of the coves that beckon along the coast to the north-east is this pohutukawa-fringed bay.*

ORUAITI CHAPEL *A pioneer memorial.*

Whangarei, the "capital" of Northland, the "winterless north", rests on the lip of the country's finest deep-water port – a feature which attracted the oil refinery to nearby Marsden Point and with it a new prosperity. The city was fortunate, too, that the decision to site the installations here was taken before the discovery of vast quantities of gas and oil condensate off the Taranaki coast, for the claims of New Plymouth might later have proved irresistible.

The rugged, jagged hills which nurse the sheltered harbour are crowned by the magnificence of Mt Manaia (403 metres), whose five peaks, silhouetted against an eastern sky, are rich in the suggestion that is the lifeblood of mythology.

Its climate and proximity to the more proclaimed enticements further north render Whangarei an exceptionally pleasant place to live, but to the visitor the lure of the north tends to obscure the generous endowments close to hand. These include deep-sea fishing at Tutukaka, bathing along an intriguing coastline, and bush walks through small stands of kauri.

SYMBOLS OF PROSPERITY *The yachts of Aucklanders mix with locally owned craft.*

TOWNSCAPE *A segment of the panorama afforded from atop Mt Parahaki.*

WHANGAREI HEADS *In the distance are the figures on Mt Manaia. In mythology a jealous husband was about to slay his eloping wife when all were turned to stone.*

Waipu A portrait of the austere leader of the Scottish Highlanders who founded the town is displayed in the museum, the "Hall of Memories". The bay, looking out to the Hen and Chicken Islands, affords excellent surfing and fishing.

Whangarei From a backwater town whose past development had been hampered by transport problems, Whangarei blossomed into a burgeoning city after it was chosen as the site for the country's oil refinery, whose flare stack at Marsden Point may be seen from afar as it burns off waste gases. An oil-fired power station followed and industries mushroomed. This sudden growth and prosperity stems from and is maintained by Whangarei's deep-water harbour, capable of handling some of the world's largest tankers. Crude oil shipped in bulk has, since 1964, been broken down here: previously, refined products had to be shipped from the Middle East – a more costly undertaking. In addition to imported crude, the refinery processes New Zealand's own condensate shipped from Taranaki.

But despite today's industrial base, with sheet glass-making, fertilizers and cement looming large, Whangarei wears a gentle air, as towering hills to east and west and a lush surrounding countryside combine to provide both a rural "feel" and a reminder of the city's recent role as little more than a farming centre. Too many travellers simply pass through in their eagerness to reach the Bay of Islands. Yet to pause is to be able to enjoy a scenic run out to Whangarei Heads, contemplate the past in the Northland Museum or the passage of time among the Clapham Clocks exhibits. Though for safety reasons the refinery cannot be visited, impressions of the magnitude of the undertaking may be gained from nearby car parks. Whangarei Falls are only five kilometres away, and there are a number of pretty parks, some with stands of kauri. The lookout on Parahaki, with its panoramic view, is easily reached, either by car or on foot through Mair Park.

CLAPHAM CLOCK MUSEUM The display of over 400 antique clocks generates a cacophony of ticks and chimes.

MARSDEN POINT *The nation's oil refinery.*

FACES OF THE NORTH *The north is home for many of New Zealand's Maoris.*

NATURE'S STATUES *Weathered limestone at the Waro reserve near Kamo.*

Hokianga Harbour

A VIEW FROM OMAPERE *Approached from the south, the Hokianga Harbour opens out with a dramatic suddenness.*

OPO AND FRIENDS The dolphin "Opo" brought world fame to tiny Opononi when, for only the second time in history and the first in nearly 2,000 years, a wild dolphin chose to befriend children in the water, cavorting with them and giving them rides.

NGAWHA HOT SPRINGS *Soda mercury pools reputed to have curative properties.*

Hokianga Harbour The harbour, a drowned river system with a hazardous bar, is one of very few natural harbours on the country's west coast. It was of considerable significance in pioneer days, when its bar claimed many vessels during the height of the kauri timber trade, and ships plied its arms as far as Horeke.

Horeke A tiny settlement on the inner reaches of the harbour, notable for the Mangungu Mission House. Originally built here in 1838, it was subsequently dismantled and removed to Onehunga to serve as a parsonage. More recently it has been returned to its original site by the Historic Places Trust.

Kohukohu A town which once dominated the harbour in size and importance has what is reputed to be the oldest bridge in the country – though certainly not the largest!

Omanaia Missionaries emphasised that "good Christian" converts not only renounced old spiritual ways, but also their material culture. Understandably, this rigidity spawned resistance, and buried in the churchyard here is Papahurihia, who led local Maori opposition. Both church (long ceased to be used as such) and burial ground are closed to visitors.

Omapere Attractive views encompass harbour, heads and the golden sand dunes that encroach on farmland. Across the water is where Kupe is reputed to have farewelled the land he had discovered.

Onoke Still standing here is the modest house of the self-styled "Pakeha-Maori", Judge Maning, an Irishman who moved here in 1833 and later helped establish the Maori Land Court.

CLENDON HOUSE Situated at Rawene, overlooking the Hokianga Harbour, this house is little changed from when it was first built in about 1860. James Clendon was a ship's master who visited the area in 1829, then traded in the Bay of Islands, where he was the United States Consul. When the country became a British colony, he sold his home at Okiato for it to become New Zealand's first Government House. It was as a Resident Magistrate that he finally came to live here, but in retirement his commercial ventures failed, and this house soon passed into his father-in-law's ownership. It is now owned by the Historic Places Trust and is open to visitors.

STANDING ON STILTS *Clusters of buildings standing on stilts over the water lend charm to both Rawene (pictured) and Horeke.*

KING OF THE KAURI *Te Matua Ngahere, the "Father of the Forest", may be as many as 2,000 years old and is one of the largest of the trees in the Waipoua Kauri Forest.*

MAXWELL'S HUT *An early bushman's hut turned museum in Waipoua Forest.*

Opononi Popular with holidaymakers for its safe bathing, good boating and plentiful fish, Opononi can be translated as meaning "place of bountiful hospitality". A monument to the dolphin "Opo" is on the seafront. Another, to Kupe, is nearby at Pakanae.

Rawene A waterside township brimful with personality (*see picture*). A ferry from here links with Kohukohu on the northern shore.

Trounson Kauri Park A stand smaller and quite different in character from Waipoua.

Waipoua Kauri Forest Over 2,500 hectares of mature kauri forest comprise the last significant stand of the tree that contributed much to the country's development. Cook had recognised its value, and before long the British Navy was here, plundering the forests for timber for shipbuilding. Early settlers, too, used it for their homes, and an export trade quickly developed. Timber was being cut very much faster than the trees could regenerate, but as the trade dwindled another took its place – gum. The kauri exudes a resin that hardens on contact with the air, and was found to have a high value in the manufacture of varnishes.

A rush followed, with many migrants, principally from Yugoslavia, pouring in to search for gum from kauri forests long departed, poking deep into the soil with long rods then digging down when the omens seemed good. In so doing they ravaged large areas of land, and desolate tracts pitted with gum holes are still to be seen in the north.

The broad and serene sweep of Hokianga Harbour contrasts starkly with the bustle of the Bay of Islands. There, history, land and sea are the stuff of commerce: here, not so very far distant, the land seems to live as much in the past as in the present and any hunger for tourist traffic seems half-hearted. Here was to be the kingdom of Baron de Thierry, "Sovereign Chief of New Zealand", but the Frenchman's grandiose schemes collapsed and he ended his days not holding court, but teaching piano in Auckland.

To the south rise the massive kauri trees of the Waipoua Forest, some venerable to the point of antiquity and easily the giants of the New Zealand forest. Here they grow more or less in their primitive environment, dwarfing the trees beneath. Their saplings, straight and lacking knots, show at a glance why it was that the British Navy was prepared to come so far to plunder them for use as masts and as spars. Indeed, the sapling's name, "ricker", is a corruption of "rigger". The main road carves through the forest for nearly 16 kilometres, with tracks to the major trees well signposted.

NORTHLAND PASTORAL *A century ago this was dense forest like the hills in the background.*

Maori myth

Maori culture is rich in myths and legends. They tell of the creation of the universe, of gods descending into humans. They describe the emergence from the sea of the land they called Aotearoa and rehearse the coming of canoes from a "Hawaiki" homeland to populate its shores.

These tales embody, in the absence of a written language, many aspects of Maori culture – customs, beliefs, knowledge, skills, religion, superstition – but above all they represent the accumulated store of experience. All that had been learnt and practised was woven into Maori oral literature, etched into carvings and mirrored in song and dance to be re-created, renewed and adapted by each generation. Inevitably, as is the nature of folklore, sources disagree, for there can never be one, single, "authentic" version.

These stories are moving and beautiful in their own right, for the Maori traditionally had a highly sophisticated command of poetic language, and a colourful rendition was itself an aid to memory. Not infrequently behind their elaborate texture lay a practical and vital purpose which formed the very cement of the Maori's culture. For example, some legends tell of Kupe, the Polynesian explorer credited with being among the first to visit the country's shores, chasing a *wheke* (octopus) all the way from Hawaiki after it had stripped bait from his fishing line. They tell of a furious encounter, in the course of which Kupe chased the octopus along the Wairarapa coast and into Cook Strait, detailing the account so minutely as to provide an oral map to the Marlborough Sounds, an important and tricky area for navigation. Another account tells of a canoe's being wrecked on the North Otago coast. Curious boulders on the beaches are described as petrified kumara and gourd seeds washed ashore; a particular reef is described as the canoe's hull, and the peaks of the ranges to the north are given the names of passengers. Even Mt Cook is given the name of a boy who was carried on his grandfather's shoulders and was thus the tallest of the survivors. The account is of an overland journey so detailed that none who knew it could be lost.

Not surprisingly (for the people share a common origin), many aspects of Maori mythology are echoed in other islands of Polynesia. Even Maui, the great fisher of land from the sea, must be shared with other island groups.

Unfortunately, if inevitably, the oral tradition was an early casualty of European settlement. New questions were asked to which new answers had to be found, and although a number of early settlers (including Sir George Grey) played a major part in preserving what they could understand of the myths and legends, they fed their own interpretations back, giving rise to such phantoms as the "Great Migration". The Europeans had migrated here *en masse*, so thought the Maori would have done likewise. Such distortions continue to this day to mar the popular understanding of historical fact.

Kaipara Harbour

OTAMATEA KAURI AND PIONEER MUSEUM *Matakohe's museum is a celebration of the kauri. Colonial furniture (below) and the largest kauri gum collection in the world (above) testify to the beauty and richness of a once great natural resource. The gum, seen here in every size, shape and colour, was much sought-after about the turn of the century. Long rods known as "gum spears" were used to prod the swamps where mighty forests had once stood; other gum was taken by climbing trees.*

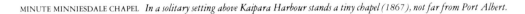

MINUTE MINNIESDALE CHAPEL *In a solitary setting above Kaipara Harbour stands a tiny chapel (1867), not far from Port Albert.*

The dairylands north-west of Auckland are probed by the long fingers of a tranquil harbour to present a scene of serenity – a happy blend of land and water.

The prospect today masks the bustle of yesteryear, when small boats hustled to and fro, ferrying kauri timber, gum and agricultural produce to the infant and fast-growing Auckland. Occasionally, too, there is the reminder of unfulfilled promise – such as at Port Albert, where a determined settlement of over 3,000 turned their hands to everything they could imagine before yielding to the dictates of an uncertain tidal harbour and a plague of crop diseases.

The area demands a lingering appreciation, a savouring at leisure of an endlessly changing relationship of sea and farmland. Perhaps its most outstanding single feature is to be found at the tiny town of Matakohe, with its unequalled collection of kauri gum and a memorial church to the country's first native-born Prime Minister.

PASTURELAND, MATAKOHE *Cabbage trees on the upper reaches of the harbour.*

Dargaville A dairying centre on the banks of the Wairoa River about 60 kilometres north of the entrance to Kaipara Harbour, Dargaville perpetuates the name of its Australian founder and serves as a jumping-off point for visits to the Waipoua and Trounson Kauri Forests to the north. The wharf recalls the town's role as a port in the heyday of the kauri timber and later gum trades. The area's history is captured by the local museum. Large tracts of land in the locality, for generations unproductive as a result of the gum digging, have been rehabilitated in recent decades. The Kai Iwi Lakes are much favoured for boating and fishing.

Helensville At the opposite end of the harbour from Dargaville lies Helensville, also a dairying centre but one named not for its founder but for a pioneer's wife. Set on a hillside above the Kaipara River, the town once had a shipping role: indeed, its principal access to Auckland (today only 50 kilometres by road) was a hazardous voyage around North Cape to the Waitemata. Hot springs at Parakai draw visitors from far afield, and a number of motels have their own thermal pools.

PARAKAI HOT POOLS *Helensville's mineral springs open all day and into the evenings.*

KERERU *The native pigeon ranks as one of the most magnificent of the species, both in size and brilliance of plumage. Its numbers have dwindled with the forests.*

COATES MEMORIAL CHURCH Twice decorated for bravery in World War I, locally born Gordon Coates is depicted in Matakohe's church as a knight in armour. As the country's first native-born Prime Minister (1925–28), he could not live up to the expectations of the electorate, but his political career continued and he made outstanding contributions both during the Depression and in the War Cabinet.

A RURAL SETTING *The main highway near Matakohe passes through rolling dairy country typical of the north.*

PAHI DOMAIN *A colossal fig tree dominates the seaside recreation ground.*

Kaipara Harbour The harbour's many arms penetrate deep into the shoreline but are little seen from the main highway. Its dangerous bar has claimed many ships, some of whose skeletons still rest on North Spit, near Pouto. The harbour's importance ended with the era of coastal shipping.

Matakohe A tiny settlement on the northern reaches, renowned for its museum and church.

Pahi A short detour from Highway 12 leads to a pleasant picnic spot, with good boating, swimming, camping – and shade from a Moreton Bay fig tree of truly gargantuan proportions.

Port Albert Now simply a cluster of houses, this was where in the 1860s a special settlement of about 3,000 Nonconformists struggled against all odds in a battle to wrest a living from the land. Their enterprise and their failure are recorded in the Albertland Museum.

Wellsford A farming centre on the neck of land which bridges Northland to Auckland.

DISUSED LIFTING BRIDGE *A relic of Dargaville's days as a coastal shipping port.*

KAURI FOREST, WAIROA RIVER, KAIPARA (1839) *Early timber-felling techniques are faithfully observed in a watercolour by the New Zealand Company surveyor-artist Charles Heaphy. Heaphy's works, noted for their draughtsmanship, command high prices more for historical than for artistic reasons. The early travellers sketched as today's take photographs.*

The Hibiscus Coast, Islands of the Hauraki Gulf

A YACHTING PARADISE *A well-laden yacht cruises on the Hauraki Gulf, whose waters are nursed by the mainland to the west and the long, northward-reaching arm of the Coromandel Peninsula to the east. Sheltered from all winds save the northerly (Hauraki means "north wind"), it is a perfect haven for boats. Many of its islands have been incorporated into the Hauraki Gulf Maritime Park.*

Paving the way north along the eastern coastline from Auckland lies a golden chain of beautiful beaches, shelving into the island-freckled reaches of the Hauraki Gulf. Such gems so close to the country's metropolis ensure the presence of numerous commuter and retirement settlements as well as, in summer, hosts of good-humoured holidaymakers.

Yet solitude, too, is near at hand. For a little inland lies tranquil, tiny Puhoi, unusual for its wayside shrine and unique for its Bohemian origins. It was to the solitude, too, of Wenderholm that the former British Prime Minister, Sir Anthony Eden, retreated for a time to recuperate from the double blows of surgery and the Suez crisis which marked both a turning point in world history and his own political demise.

The Gulf itself, almost landlocked by Great and Little Barrier Islands, is a fabled fishing ground and a paradise for boats large and small. Across its waters, passenger ferries and swift launches whisk commuters and visitors to a scattering of homes and remote picnic and camping places.

Hauraki Gulf Maritime Park The park takes in dozens of islands which, by purchase, gift or transfer from local bodies, have been amalgamated with areas already owned by the Crown to establish a maritime park. The islands and their uses vary. Some are so remote and inaccessible that they are unsuited for recreation but ideal for the study of wildlife and the preservation both of bird species and of the small relic populations of the reptile tuatara. Others are reached more easily and are picturesque settings for holiday outings. Their histories, too, are varied. Rangitoto, youngest of the islands, is enshrined in Maori legend; Browns Island was farmed by the partners Campbell and Brown who foresaw the birth of Auckland; Motuihe has served both as a quarantine station and prisoner-of-war camp, and North Head, the only part of the mainland included in the park, preserves a long-time military fort with emplacements dating from every time of crisis, real or imaginary, since 1885.

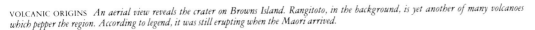

VOLCANIC ORIGINS *An aerial view reveals the crater on Browns Island. Rangitoto, in the background, is yet another of many volcanoes which pepper the region. According to legend, it was still erupting when the Maori arrived.*

CLEMATIS *One of about nine endemic species.*

KAWAU ISLAND *Mansion House (c. 1862), the creation of an early Governor, Sir George Grey, who later became Prime Minister, has been restored within and without, by the Hauraki Gulf Maritime Park Board. Much visited by private boats, the island is also accessible by ferry from Sandspit, near Warkworth.*

BOHEMIAN ORIGINS Puhoi's history reflected in stained glass.

East Coast Bays Auckland's northern suburbs string out along a series of close, east-facing bays.

Great and Little Barrier Islands The two islands that guard the entrance to the Gulf could not be more different: geologically Great Barrier is a detached piece of the Coromandel Peninsula while Little Barrier is a volcanic cone of comparatively recent origin. Great Barrier supports a small permanent population and is visited by holidaymakers; Little Barrier, virtually untouched by humans or by browsing animals, is a protected wildlife sanctuary.

Kawau Island A delightful corner of the Gulf, with Grey's gracious Mansion House and imposing gardens. Wallabies he introduced are now widespread and the occasional kookaburra may also be heard.

Orewa A tranquil seaside town with a statue of Sir Edmund Hillary. In summer it assumes a more hectic pace as holidaymakers descend to swell the town to the size of a small, bustling city.

Waiheke Island The largest and most settled of the Gulf's islands, it has a variety of sheltered bays and offers excellent fishing.

Waiwera Aside from the beach, which is akin to Orewa, attractions are enhanced by hot springs and the extensive Wenderholm Reserve.

Warkworth A farming centre distinguished by the country's satellite station. Close by is Mahurangi Peninsula, less populated than Whangaparaoa and

SANDSPIT *A launching place for runabouts on the Mahurangi Peninsula.*

PUHOI'S PUB *Relics and photographs of Puhoi's colourful past lend the hotel an atmosphere all its own.*

with fine beaches. Diving is a popular sport here, and access to Kawau Island is from Sandspit.

Whangaparaoa Peninsula Very closely settled and within commuting distance of Auckland, the peninsula compensates with a myriad of inlets which ensure that, whatever the breeze, a sheltered swimming spot can be found.

SPACE LINK *One of the antennae of Warkworth's satellite station.*

STITCHBIRD The stitchbird belongs to the "honey-eater" family which also includes the tui and bellbird. Unlike the others, found throughout the country, this native bird is now found only on Little Barrier Island. The name refers not to nest-building but to its high-pitched call. The Maori once hunted the birds for food and used its yellow feathers in the manufacture of cloaks.

PALM BEACH *A sheltered resort on the northern side of Waiheke Island.*

Auckland

A CITY OF THE SEA *Spanning the waters of the Waitemata to link the suburbs of the North Shore with the heart of Auckland city is the Harbour Bridge, recently widened to accommodate increasing traffic.*

In the country's metropolis a population of a million sprawls over an area larger than that of Greater London. Washed by twin seas, flanked by twin harbours, the city is characterised by many volcanic cones, the thousands of yachts that speckle its bays and a vigorous outdoor lifestyle. Its ethos, too, is more assertive than is found elsewhere.

As well as being the uncrowned capital of New Zealand (a title it officially enjoyed from 1840–65 and whose removal may now be seen as an unintended act of decentralisation), the city is acknowledged as being the "capital" of Polynesia, as it is now the home of more Polynesian Islanders than any other centre. This has brought with it problems of integration for Islander and New Zealander alike, but also adds the cosmopolitan riches of ethnic variety which the country's other cities largely lack.

Auckland's growth, and the "drift to the north" generally, have posed major economic problems for more southerly regions. Two-thirds of the country's population now lives north of Lake Taupo, conferring on Auckland a degree of economic domination that imperils more distant industries. Those to the south may mock the bustle, describing the city as "Little Sydney" (which in many ways it resembles), but they also acknowledge that those transferred here quickly succumb to its special charm.

QUEEN STREET BUSTLE *Pedestrians criss-cross the main street's intersection with Wellesley Street.*

26

OFF TO THE ISLANDS *The Waiheke ferry departs for the islands of the Hauraki Gulf*

OUTDOOR LIVING *A restaurant in High Street exemplifies Aucklanders' addiction to sun and fresh air.*

A city of volcanoes Auckland rests on the narrow isthmus of Tamaki Peninsula. On either side spread the generous harbours of Waitemata and Manukau, which all but sever the North Island in two. Both are river valleys formed during the last ice age and drowned when the sea's waters rose. The character of the shoreline along the open sea contrasts starkly. The wild coast to the west, characterised by titanium-rich black sand which becomes uncomfortably hot on a sunny summer's day, is pounded by the rollers of the Tasman Sea while that to the east enjoys the shelter of the Coromandel Peninsula. Though this has led to Auckland being characterised as a "city of the seas", it is pre-eminently one of volcanoes. Among the more than sixty craters that pockmark the terrain, several are prominent landmarks: One Tree Hill, with its lonely tree and obelisk; Lake Pupuke at Takapuna; Mount Eden; Mount Albert; the Waitakeres, and the graceful island cone of Rangitoto that seems to sweep into every eastwards seascape. Each evidences the fury with which the isthmus was formed. The ther-

mal springs at Helensville and elsewhere not far distant hint that the process may not yet have ended.

"The spouse of a hundred lovers" The isthmus takes its name from the Maori name, Tamaki-makau-rau, "the spouse contested by a hundred lovers", not for reasons of promiscuity but to reflect the keen way in which its possession was contested among tribes in the region. Maori legend tells of battle after battle, giving the isthmus as frenzied a history under human habitation as it had had during its formation. Almost every volcanic cone was fortified, pre-eminent being the pa on One Tree Hill, but even these massive fortifications were, on occasion, successfully attacked and laid waste. Today, traces of the various pa may be seen on Mount Eden and Mount Albert as well as on the steep slopes of One Tree Hill.

The isthmus gradually became untenable with the emergence of Ngapuhi as the country's strongest tribe early in the nineteenth century. Based in the Bay of Islands, Ngapuhi roamed south with in-

creasing frequency and daring as they gained guns from visiting whaling ships. The local population dwindled further in the face of epidemics, and by the time the isthmus was chosen to be the first substantive capital, in 1840, it was virtually deserted.

Once upon a capital ... Unlike the other "main" centres of Wellington, Christchurch and Dunedin, Auckland was not a "planned" settlement, fed with migrants arriving regularly from Britain. Rather it was the arbitrary creation of the first governor, Hobson, shortly after he had concluded the Treaty of Waitangi. Hobson's choice infuriated the New Zealand Company, who had anticipated that its settlement at Wellington would be preferred, and it bombarded the British Government with objections and complaints. But the Governor's choice was well made. Anxious to prevent strife between Maori and Pakeha, he had selected a site which was easily defended and which effectively severed the two major areas of

LANDMARK *One Tree Hill and monument.*

Maori population, of which about three-quarters was living north of Lake Taupo. He had noted the ease of communication by water, ready access to essential stands of forest and the agricultural potential of the red volcanic soil. Important, too, in the choice was the initial absence of Europeans, Auckland being declared capital at a time when its Pakeha population numbered just two. One of the pair, Sir John Logan Campbell, lived to greet as Mayor the Duke and Duchess of Cornwall on their royal tour of 1901.

A VARIED ARCHITECTURE *The construction of the new is matched by the energetic refurbishment of the old. From left: part of the university; a hair salon off Queen Street; Vulcan Lane; modern high-rise.*

RUN FOR FUN   *The annual "round the bays" run draws well over 60,000 entries. Joggers and serious athletes alike are encountered at every turn.*

THE FACE OF JUSTICE? *Gargoyles embellish the High Court in Waterloo Quadrant.*

A capital denied Auckland was to enjoy just 25 years as the country's capital. During that time the city grew and prospered, partly at the expense of the Maori tribes to the south, whose land was acquired after bloodshed followed their refusal to sell voluntarily, and partly as a consequence of the presence of British troops. When these departed the economy sagged, and the settlement's plight was aggravated by the unbridled opulence of Dunedin, booming as a result of gold strikes. By then Dunedin was the commercial and entrepreneurial heart of the country, and it threatened secession if the capital was not moved south. Dunedin's apparent intransigence is the more understandable when one appreciates that at the time the most speedy line of communication with the then capital was by way of Sydney. Before long, in 1865, the capital was moved to Welling-

ton, and Auckland's fortunes ebbed lower still. Too late, the gold that had robbed Auckland of her crown restored her fortunes – fabulous finds were made on the Coromandel Peninsula, just across the Hauraki Gulf, and these revived the commercial instincts in the Aucklanders which have never since flagged.

Today Auckland's domination over the country is near total. This continues to grow as the magnet of its large population (and so its workforce and its markets) attracts ever-increasing industry at the expense of less well-populated regions to the south. Major industrial activities include the manufacture of clothing, footwear, foodstuffs, domestic appliances, textiles, furnishings and building materials. As well as having more heavy industry than any other centre, it is also home to engineering and allied trades.

SHEEP IN THE CITY'S HEART *A view of Cornwall Park.*

STRAND ARCADE *One of several shopping arcades adjoining Queen Street.*

PARNELL VILLAGE *A cluster of boutiques in a Victorian setting in Parnell Road.*

OMINOUS REMINDER The rifle slits of Albert Barracks (1846–52), near Albert Park, mark the tempestuous beginnings of the colony.

RESTAURANTS PROLIFERATE *A typical "new" restaurant at Herne Bay.*

A FASCINATION FOR THE SEA *Thousands of boats are owned by Aucklanders; others are for hire. Still more are taking shape in garages and back gardens. The Anniversary Day Regatta (January) is billed as the world's largest.*

ANIMALS FROM THE WORLD OVER Auckland's Zoological Gardens, the country's most comprehensive, also house native animals and boast a nocturnal kiwi house. The animals are fed in the afternoons.

The city's heart The city's principal street, Queen Street, flanked by some of the country's largest departmental stores, dips gently downhill to meet the harbour. From the waterfront is seen Auckland's Harbour Bridge – over 1,000 metres of steel spanning the Waitemata Harbour to link the increasingly popular North Shore directly to the downtown area. Inevitably its design earns the nickname, "the coat-hanger", while the Japanese-built extensions adding additional lanes on either side are known as the "Nippon clip-ons". Cutting across the upper reaches of Queen Street is Karangahape Road, Auckland's counterpart to Sydney's Kings Cross, where the varied ethnic origins of the city's multi-cultural population are best appreciated. Only two blocks from Queen Street and adjoining the oldest buildings of the University of Auckland, is Albert Park, popular with lunchtime office workers. The park marks the site of the Albert Barracks, built in 1846 in Auckland's early

tainty. Only the rifle-slit walls behind the university's administration building have survived. From the foot of Queen Street numerous launches leave to cruise the island-scattered waters of the Hauraki Gulf on what is, for some, a commuter run. For those with less time, or who would also see the city from the air, amphibious flights leave from Mechanics Bay.

A POLYNESIAN BANQUET ... *but held indoors.*

PONSONBY GRAFFITI *Murals add colour to inner-city architecture.*

HOBSON'S GRAVE *The country's first Governor lies in the old Symonds Street cemetery.*

ALBERTON This romantic 18-roomed colonial mansion dates from 1862 and is furnished in the period *(100 Mount Albert Road; open daily).*

AUCKLAND WAR MEMORIAL MUSEUM In the parkland setting of the Domain, the Museum covers the general disciplines of zoology, botany and ethnology. A large display is devoted to the two world wars. Particularly strong sections concern the Maori and the Pacific. *Below from left*: Kawe, a Caroline Islands goddess; a carved wooden Buddha (c. 1450A.D.); a pre-European Maori carving.

Volcanic viewpoints Some of the smaller volcanic cones have been quarried out of existence for their scoria. The three largest, however, have been preserved as scenic reserves, and each offers a magnificent and somewhat different panorama. One Tree Hill is topped with a towering column to celebrate Sir John Logan Campbell's admiration for the Maori people, while at the base of the obelisk the Founder Citizen of Auckland lies buried. Somewhat higher is Mount Eden (196 metres), with a view which encompasses the whole of the Auckland isth-

CELEBRATING THE HARVEST *Dancers in traditional Dalmatian costume mingle with more conventionally attired visitors at Auckland's annual Wine Festival. A number of major vineyards are near the city.*

GREER TWISS SCULPTURE *In Karangahape Road.*

mus. Mount Albert, marginally less spectacular, like the others is plainly marked with the earthworks of fortified pa. Its green slopes contrast sharply with surrounding suburbia.

Varied museums and art galleries
The Auckland War Memorial Museum, in a parkland setting, ranks with the country's best and has a particularly splendid display of early Maori material. "Journey's End" Cottage and Museum, built as a Fencible cottage, recalls Onehunga's origins as a fencible settle-

ment, one of a chain of settlements established to secure the infant Auckland from attack by surrounding it with military settlers (*Jellicoe Park*). The roomy kauri cottage of an early cleric, Ewelme Cottage (1863-64) contains much original furniture (*Ayr Street, Parnell*) and contrasts with the grandeur of the colonial mansion of Alberton (*Mt Albert Road*). The ingenuity of Kelly Tarlton's Underwater World (*Tamaki Drive*) fascinates all. In totally different vein is the Museum of Transport and Technology (*Great North Road, Western Springs*) but even this augments computers, steam engines and a fine array of aircraft with a pioneer village to preserve interesting colonial buildings that might otherwise have been demolished. The museum is of special interest on "Live Weekends", when everything that can move does.

The city is a major centre for artists, and their work is to be found for sale in the many private galleries that abound, as well as in the Auckland City Art Gallery (*cnr Kitchener and Wellesley Streets*), which also has a good collection of Gothic art.

CRAFT MARKET *Potters, weavers, silversmiths, woodworkers and leatherworkers ply their trade in Brown's Mill, off Darby Street.*

MISSION BAY BEACH *The scene of early missionary endeavour is now given over to summertime leisure.*

WAITAKERE RANGES *Native bush softens the volcanic origins of the hills.*

Interesting buildings Auckland's beginnings are remembered in the 120 hectares of Cornwall Park, where Acacia cottage (1841), built as John Logan Campbell's early home, has been moved onto the land he once farmed. St Stephen's Chapel (1856–57) was where the constitution for the Church of the Province of New Zealand was signed in 1857 (*off St Stephens Avenue, Parnell*). Also in Parnell is a pleasing cluster of ecclesiastical buildings which includes Selwyn Court (1863), the Cathedral Church of St Mary (1888) and the modern Holy Trinity Cathedral (*cnr St Stephens Avenue and Parnell Road*), as well as the Victorian cottage shopping complex of Parnell Village (*259 Parnell Road*).

Choice beaches The choice lies between the wild, ocean-swept beaches of the west coast (personified as male by the Maori) and those of the sheltered east coast (personified as female). To the west, Piha (the most popular) (*40 km*), Muriwai (*43 km*) and Whatipu (*44 km*) each has its devotees, with Whatipu offering the safest bathing. The inner-harbour beaches are, of course, more affected by the tide, but Mission Bay is of special appeal. To the north, along the east coast, lies a chain of beaches from North Head to the much-indented shore-line of the Whangaparaoa Peninsula (*37 km*). Farther north are the seaside resorts of Orewa (*40 km*) and Waiwera (*48 km*), the latter's beach being augmented with thermal pools.

Some other essentials: At Kelly Tarlton's Underwater World an acrylic tunnel leads under the sea for a fish-eye view of marine life (*Orakei Wharf, Tamaki Drive*). Above ground, a Maori concert party entertains at the N.Z. Heritage Park, where varied facets of the nation's life are on display (*Harrison Road, Mt Wellington*). For comic strip devotees the Footrot Flats Leisure Park beckons (*Te Atatu*), and for the more intrepid a heart-stopping roller-coaster awaits at Rainbows End Adventure Park (*Manukau City*). Henderson *18 km NW* is the centre of a flourishing wine district, and Howick (*22 km*) recalls its origins as a military settlement.

PIONEER AVIATOR *With empty tins and a collection of farmyard bits and pieces, Richard Pearse (1877–1953) almost succeeded in racing the Wright brothers into the air. The inventive genius of this South Canterbury eccentric is displayed at the Museum of Transport and Technology, Western Springs.*

A "SELWYN" CHAPEL The tiny St Stephen's Chapel in Parnell, in whose churchyard many Auckland pioneers lie buried.

A SURFER'S PARADISE *North of Piha.*

SUNRISE *Day breaks over the city and the Westhaven marina.*

South Auckland

IRON HORSE *At Glenbrook a vintage railway recalls technology before the steel mills.*

FOOD FOR A CITY *Pukekohe's prodigious market gardens and farmlands have fed Auckland for over a century.*

Bombay A farming hamlet on Highway 1, Bombay is as far removed from its Indian namesake in character as it is in distance. Its name derives from that of an early immigrant ship and lends itself to that of the Pukewau Range, now more familiarly the Bombay Hills, which mark the boundary between the Auckland and Waikato regions. Here market gardening is pre-eminent. Roadside stalls tempt the passing motorist while fields of seasonal vegetables, fruit and horticultural produce spread out in an ever-changing chequerboard of brown and green.

Drury A rapidly growing industrial and commercial centre, Drury is typical of several South Auckland townships whose sturdy rural heritage has changed dramatically in the last few decades. Strategically placed at the head of an inlet on the Manukau Harbour and also on the Great South Road (now designated Highway 1), its former role as a vital supply depot for troops fighting in the Waikato has a modern equivalent in the supply of industrial goods for the national and export markets.

Glenbrook From quiet obscurity the locality was plunged into national focus by the decision to site the country's sole steel mill here. The mill exploits some of the potential of the vast quantities of ironsand found on a number of west coast beaches.

South of the metropolis of Auckland the land fans out wide and prosperous, with essential dairylands and market gardens. The "threat" to the area (if such it can be called) today lies in the expanding city to the north, but much of the fascination in its past derives from a threat to the south — from dispossessed Maori tribes and the establishment more than a century ago of "pensioner" or "Fencible" settlements as an outer defensive screen for the then-capital. Granted land in return for light military duties, former Imperial soldiers, specially recruited and brought here, divided their time between guarding the burgeoning town of Auckland and growing food to feed it. Howick, Onehunga, Panmure and Otahuhu were all born in this fashion.

To the south, beyond the Bombay Hills, lies the abundance of the Waikato.

NEW ZEALAND'S GATEWAY *For most overseas visitors, their first contact with the country is at Mangere International Airport.*

PAKURANGA *An aerial view of residential development in an expanding Auckland.*

FENCIBLE COTTAGE *History at Howick.*

PUKEKOHE GRAND PRIX The country's premier motor race is held here annually.

GLENBROOK STEEL *From scrap and iron-sand the material for industrial processing.*

Howick A seaside commuter suburb of Auckland, Howick still retains something of a village atmosphere. This dates from its founding in 1847 by Fencibles who began the work of taming the landscape while guarding Auckland against the possibility of attack. Fragments surviving from these times are Shamrock Cottage (*Selwyn Road*), The Garden of Memories (*Uxbridge Street*) and All Saints' Church (*Selwyn Road*).

Manukau city One of the country's newer cities, Manukau is the product of the population explosion experienced by Auckland in the aftermath of World War II and later.

Pakuranga Until quite recently a farming and fruit-growing area, the town has mushroomed to accommodate a growing Auckland. The Lloyd Elsmore Park (*Bells Road*) preserves a number of elegant and historic old buildings, including one of only two two-storeyed Fencible cottages (moved here in 1895).

Papakura Another of the early frontier towns, Papakura preserves a military link in its large Army camp. The picturesque Hunua Falls are only about 16 kilometres away, and at Pukekiwiriki pa site (*Red Hill Road*) there is a magnificent panor-

ama as well as a fine example of a pre-European pa.

Pokeno Here there is an old military cemetery and a stone memorial to those who died near here in 1863. Queen's Redoubt, a major establishment, was sited about 400 metres away.

Pukekohe Extensive market gardens take full advantage of the rich volcanic soil, but dairying and sheep farming also loom large. A particularly appealing view over the town and countryside is gained from Pukekohe Hill. Curiosities include two once-fortified and battle-scarred churches, Pukekohe East Presbyterian Church and St Brides, Mauku. Each January the town experiences the excitement of the New Zealand Grand Prix.

ALL SAINTS', HOWICK (1847) *One of several distinctive churches built around Auckland by Bishop Seluyn, Anglican primate of New Zealand from 1842–68.*

Sport

A passion for sport runs deep in the nation's psyche, drawing on the colonists' competitive nature and their genius for co-operation. Perhaps no other country of comparable size sets for itself such high standards, or has produced as many champions. At the Olympic Games, middle-distance runners – Lovelock, Halberg, Snell, Walker – have passed into legend; rowing-eights and yachtsmen have defeated the world's best, and even a lowly ranked hockey team has returned with gold medals. Denis Hulme has won the world motor-racing drivers' championship; Edmund Hillary was the first to scale Everest; Timaru-reared Bob Fitzsimmons held the world heavy-weight boxing crown; Clark McConachy defeated all comers at billiards; Anthony Wilding won ten Wimbledon tennis titles, and even the country's seldom-fancied cricketers have scored wins over all the major cricket-playing nations.

Despite the variety of these successes ,and the determined and dedicated followings that a plethora of sports enjoy, rugby union continues to dominate the public consciousness, though today not as totally as once was the case. Only in the valleys of Wales is a similar religious fervour encountered.

There, rivalry was sparked from the outset when, in their first encounter in 1905, the All Blacks were robbed of victory by an inept referee – a contentious defeat which still rankles whenever the sides clash, but one which has been more than avenged by a lengthy, unbroken string of All Black victories. The passion for rugby is challenged only by a fondness for horse-racing, and government-owned betting shops (TABs) ensure that this is a profitable pastime for the taxpayer as well as for the jockey clubs.

Away from the sports fields, countless numbers of New Zealanders jog endlessly along city streets and country roads, many in training for particular sports, but most simply for the joy of running. In such an atmosphere "new" sports have emerged. The country can lay claim to having originated the sports of girls' marching, wood chopping and competitive sheep-shearing. At this last, New Zealand shearers have swept the boards, while in the country's woolsheds, upwards of 500 sheep have on occasions been shorn in a single day by just one man.

Apart from competitive sports and as befits a people come to escape the gamekeeper and his laird and to deny any property in wild game, there is excellent trout fishing throughout the country, good salmon in some rivers, and wild pigs and goats to shoot. Deer, once plentiful, now prove elusive as their numbers in the ranges have been run down with the boom in deer farming. Big-game fish can be taken from boats off the east coast of Northland and the Bay of Plenty, where several world records have been set. The *Guinness Book of Records* also attributed to a Mayor Island boat the longest individual fight, when a huge broadbill was played for over 32 hours and the boat towed fully 50 kilometres before the line eventually snapped – the "one that got away" that still made the record book!

In exhilarating vein, too, are the many white water rafting expeditions, which test the nerve of even the most intrepid as they splash down foaming mountain rivers. There is excellent skiing on Ruapehu, and some on Mount Egmont.

Coromandel Peninsula

A BEACH IN MERCURY BAY *North of Whitianga the Coromandel landscape offers something for everyone: shining sand, brilliant sea, steep cliffs and both pasturelands and native bush competing for the hills.*

WHITIANGA'S FISHING BOATS *Trevally, snapper and tarakihi are caught along the coast.*

The Coromandel Peninsula juts like a giant claw from the South Auckland coastline to cleave the Hauraki Gulf from the Pacific Ocean. To the east, the Pacific provides a series of splendid surf beaches, while to the west lie the sheltered waters of the Gulf. Between, the peninsula rises wild, rugged and high – remarkably so for its comparatively narrow width – reflecting starkly its volcanic origins. Extensive bush reserves cover the mountainous ranges forming the peninsula's backbone. Forest tracks are popular with the walker, many studded with relics of early kauri-felling and gold-mining days. Kauri timber, gum and gold drew men to the Coromandel in the last century. Today the peninsula serves a dual farming and recreational role.

It is the beauty of the scenery, with its sandy beaches and overhanging pohutukawa trees, that attracts holidaymakers every year to Coromandel. Swimming, boating, fishing and waterskiing are popular on both coasts. Areas like Pauanui, virtually uninhabited a few years ago, are now blossoming resorts with a growing holiday population.

EARLY GOLD-MINING MACHINERY *Relics on the Karangahake field, Ohinemuri River.*

SEASIDE SPRINGS Hot water is where your toes find it – on Hot Water Beach. The springs seep through the sand, which can be scooped out at low tide to provide an open-air bath tub.

HAHEI BEACH One of the two once-fortified Maori pa sites at the south-eastern end of Hahei Beach. The beach below is tinted pink by millions of fragments of shell. Walks lead to blow-holes, an awesome spectacle when a heavy sea is running, and to the vast cavern, carved out by the sea and named Cathedral Cave.

Cooks Beach It was on this hospitable stretch of shoreline in Mercury Bay, across from Whitianga, that Captain Cook observed the transit of Mercury (he had previously observed the transit of Venus in Tahiti). While he was ashore making his observations, a strange group of Maori rowed out to the ship to trade. When one refused to return a piece of cloth, he was shot and killed – an event which troubled Cook "because I thought the punishment a little too severe for the Crime". Six days later he formally displayed "English Colours" and took possession of the North Island.

Coromandel Forest Park The park spreads over nearly 70,000 hectares of the peninsula, affording excellent tramping. Hidden in the hills are a number of dams, originally built to trap water which was released suddenly to

VICTORIAN PUB *Thames has a number of classic wooden colonial buildings.*

sweep kauri logs down towards the coast. Some areas of kauri forest still survive, and in others the forest giant, now protected, is slowly regenerating.

Hahei An attractive, unusually coloured beach with walks to blow-holes, pa sites and majestic Cathedral Cave.

Mount Moehau A strenuous seven-hour climb to the highest point on the Moehau Range, near the peninsula's tip, leads to the most spectacular of panoramas.

Ohinemuri River Gold workings between Paeroa and Waihi are attracting increasingly large numbers of visitors.

Paeroa On the edge of the Hauraki Plains and technically in the Waikato, Paeroa is renowned for the drink once made from local mineral water and still marketed nationally as "Lemon and Paeroa". Close by, on the Waihou River, the Historical Maritime Park restores and displays venerable sail and steam ships.

SHAGS *A very elegant species.*

Coromandel The township is redolent with nostalgia: today's quiet, pretty farming and holiday settlement once seethed with gold miners and echoed to the perpetual thump of gold batteries as the white quartz was pounded to surrender its metal. Not that all the gold has gone, for on Tokatea Hill above the township, and from where there is a stunning view out over the peninsula and the Hauraki Gulf, pockets of gold-flecked quartz may still be seen. Indeed, the problem of extraction disillusioned the get-rich-quick miners, who soon moved on and denied to the field's finder the Government's reward for the country's first "payable" goldfield. The essentially Victorian architecture and public buildings dating from mining days are testimony to the township's sudden birth and comparative lack of renewal. There is good camping, picnicking and safe (if tidal) bathing at nearby Long Beach.

FORMER ASSAY HOUSE *One of several historic sites in the township.*

THE COROMANDEL COASTLINE *A view of the peninsula's softer face, turned towards the gentle shelf of the Hauraki Gulf.*

37

WHITIANGA FERRY *It runs regularly across the Narrows to Ferry Landing.*

STRIKING GOLD *A steady hand and a little concentration can be rewarded with colours at Karangahake.*

KIWI INGENUITY A local example, suggesting that the New Zealander may be refining, rather than losing, the knack for improvisation. Farming communities throughout the world have traditions of resourcefulness, but in few countries has this been transported so firmly into the towns.

Tairua A recently developed beach resort backed by the Tairua Forest, stretching up into the peninsula's jagged spine.

Thames The town literally mushroomed when amazing finds of gold were made in 1867. Today the peninsula's principal centre, Thames is hard to picture as a prospering and feverish settlement almost twice the size of Auckland and completely landlocked by belligerent tribes. For over a decade its only access was by sea, with ships trading across the Gulf from a depressed Auckland whose fortunes received a much-needed boost from the gold. Much of the metal was embedded in quartz, and in the early 1870s there were almost 700 stamper batteries thumping day and night, their constant hammering providing a continuous background to daily life. The winnings

were considerable, one claim in a single year returning almost $2 million. The town quickly assumed a look of substance that has long survived the gold, which had virtually dried up by 1924. Its late Victorian architecture is highly regarded, most noticeably in a number of hotels – the Lady Bowen, Brian Boru and Cornwall Arms. Gold-mining relics abound, including the School of Mines complex (which includes a major mineralogical museum), the Queen of Beauty pump (a massive device, once the largest in the Southern Hemisphere, which provided common drainage to underground workings), a gold battery (still in working order, used by local enthusiasts who continue to work their claims more as a hobby than out of hope) and the local historical museum. The hills behind the town are still, as described in 1868,

MINER'S HUT *An Ohinemuri curio shop.*

"pierced with innumerable tunnels that very much resemble an immense rabbit warren".

Thames (taking its name from the nearby river which Captain Cook compared to London's) today has a solid heavy-engineering base which stems directly from the need for heavy equipment to extract the gold, a need which saw Thames, together with neighbouring Waihi, become the first of the country's industrialised towns. Although interest in gold persists, greater numbers do better by fossicking for gemstones on a richly endowed peninsula.

WHITE-FRONTED TERNS *The species is common around the New Zealand coast.*

WHANGAMATA BEACH *The beach is highly regarded for its surf, attracting surfboard riders from all over the country.*

TAIRUA WHARF *A local fishing spot.*

COROMANDEL POTTERY *Local handicrafts, especially pottery made from nearby clay deposits, flourish in a region renowned for its uniquely "alternative" lifestyle.*

AN OLD HOMESTEAD *On the peninsula, perhaps more than elsewhere, an old-fashioned lifestyle lingers. Many former city-dwellers now live here permanently.*

Waihi Beach Planned for retiring gold miners, Waihi is a major resort with an excellent beach.

Waihi Like Thames, the town was born of gold fever and its present-day activities have an engineering base, but here it is lightweight electronics. On the hill above the town are relics of the Martha Mine, which closed only in 1953: pundits had thought that the town might die with the mine, but farming development and the introduction of television assured survival. Martha, one of the world's richest mines, produced 225 million grams of gold and 1,680 million grams of silver. The mine, which may reopen, is featured in the town's museum.

Martha Lake formed when the open-cast section of the diggings was abandoned.

Whangamata A top surfing resort, the quiet town is transformed each summer holidays. There are skindiving and fishing trips. The nearby Wentworth Valley, favoured by rockhounds, has bushed picnic spots and swimming holes.

Whitianga In an attractive setting which offers safe and easy anchorage, the summer resort looks out on island-flecked Mercury Bay. Kupe is reputed to have called here, and Cook did, describing in detail the magnificent fortified pa that stood on Whitianga Rock, across the Narrows at Ferry Landing. Big-game fishing charters may be arranged.

TAIRUA   *A holiday town in a superb setting beside the Pacific Ocean, enhanced by Paku – a twin-coned, pa-sculptured hillside that was once an island.*

Waikato

A STUD FARM NEAR CAMBRIDGE *The Waikato's consistent ability to produce champion racehorses is a source of both wonder and envy.*

TEMPLE VIEW *The Mormon temple.*

The lush, fertile Waikato wears a mantle of wealth unsurpassed elsewhere. Here graze some of the finest dairy herds; here bloodstock with revered names foal the next generation of Pacific horse-racing champions; here the country's longest river provides much of the North Island's electricity as well as some superb freshwater lakes for water-skiing, rowing and trout fishing.

The prospect, however, has changed markedly over the years. If envious settlers succeeded in what some historians would see as a straightforward war of conquest to wrest by force the fertile river flats that Waikato Maoris would not sell, the settlers' success brought hardship with it. Much of the region was swampy and the Government, impoverished by wars, had little capital to finance essential drainage. Only in the 1900s did the countryside assume its soft, tamed countenance, with scarcely a vestige of unworked land.

European farming techniques.

The city's destiny still lies with the land, and its role as an agricultural research centre is formidable: the quality of research undertaken here has brought breakthroughs in a variety of fields. The University of Waikato, too, enjoys a high reputation.

A paddleboat now cruises the Waikato, and there are delightful walks along its banks. The Waikato Art Museum illustrates pre-European life in the district, and at Mystery Creek the Clydesdale Agricultural Museum portrays the country's dairy industry. Nearby is the Mormon centre of Temple View.

LEAFY CAMBRIDGE *Exotic rather than native trees give Cambridge a special character.*

Cambridge A town of trees with a village green, Cambridge comes close to the Englishness its founders sought. Nearby is Lake Karapiro, venue for the 1978 World Rowing Championships and the farthest downstream of the Waikato hydro lakes.

Hamilton Girthed by some of the richest farmland and intersected by the broad, limpid Waikato River, Hamilton has blossomed in recent years from a modest market town to the country's largest inland city. Today's peaceful scene masks generations of struggle. In 1863 the settlers invaded the region from the north and gunboats swept up the river, ostensibly to protect infant Auckland but in reality to seize rich land from tribes who refused to sell it. (The hulk of the gunboat Rangiriri stands in Memorial Park.) The following year Hamilton was founded as a military settlement, with soldiers being paid off with confiscated land, and the task began of clearing and draining land for

LAKE KARAPIRO *The internationally acclaimed site of several major rowing championships, 12 kilometres from Hamilton.*

TE RAPA MILK POWDER FACTORY *Among the world's most modern factories, the result of farmer co-operation.*

GREENHOOD ORCHID *A wild orchid of the genus* Pterostylis.

Huntly The country's largest coalmining centre has a massive coal-and-gas-fired power station whose maximum output of 1,000 megawatts is fully 50 percent greater than that of the Waikato's eight hydro stations combined.

Matamata For many visitors the wealth of the surrounding area is eclipsed by its relaxing thermal pools.

Mercer A small riverside settlement dwarfed by the giant, belching chimneys of the coal-fired generators of Meremere power station. Close to the station are the earthworks of a pa which saw a major encounter in 1863. The base of Mercer's war memorial, once a gaol, began as a gun turret on a Waikato riverboat.

Morrinsville Centre of an area of prodigious productivity, its present prosperity conceals a lengthy struggle to drain the swamps that defeated many Waikato settlers. Close by is the Rukumoana pa, where for a time the Kingmakers of the Maori King Movement would meet.

Ngaruawahia Ngaruawahia hosts the much venerated marae of the Maori Queen with its elaborately carved buildings. The Waikato tribes sought to unify disparate Maori tribes into a single people in order to resist the advances of landhungry and well-armed settlers, but a number of key tribes opted instead to side with the Europeans and thus settle old and outstanding scores. The Waikato and Waipapa Rivers merge here, the setting for an annual regatta each March, at which are featured canoe races and hilarious canoe-hurdling.

Raglan The Waikato's beach resort has sheltered, safe waters in its harbour and sand dunes whose iron content renders them both black and blisteringly hot in the summer sun.

Te Aroha Until recently, lead and zinc were won from Te Aroha Mountain, which looms large above the town. Te Aroha, charmingly named "the loved one", was once a fashionable Victorian spa, and its quaint Tourist Gardens seem

YEARLING SALE *Hamilton's annual sales see keen competition for some of New Zealand's most promising foals.*

to belong in the pages of a Victorian scrapbook. The waters (and the hot pools) may still be taken.

Te Awamutu A pleasant farming town which presides over the southern Waikato. In its small but well-presented museum is Uenuku, an ancient wood

carving said to have accompanied a migratory canoe to New Zealand some six centuries ago.

Te Kauwhata State-owned vineyards here conduct research to increase further the quality of the country's expanding wine industry.

MERCER *Gun turret turned memorial.*

HUNTLY COAL Huntly's coal mines feed the Meremere power station and produce about 90 per cent of the nation's coal – in 1979, nearly 1.1 million tonnes of the 1.2 millions produced nationally. The coal is mined largely by open-cast methods from the drained portions of the bed of Lake Kimihia, but underground mining techniques are also used.

FITZGERALD GLADE *Stands of native bush near Tirau enrich an often exotic landscape.*

The King Country

FROM FOREST TO FARM *The familiar aspect of the region's rolling hill-country farms belies their former status as forest.*

GLOW-WORM *A pinhead light with a tiny thread.*

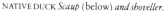

NATIVE DUCK *Scaup* (below) *and shoveller.*

WAITOMO CAVES The fantasy of limestone formations found in the series of caves at Waitomo provides a unique experience. The walks in the caves, which are cleverly lit to highlight special features, are enhanced by the gloom and enlivened by the occasional and unexpected drip of water on the nape of one's neck. Crowning all is the journey on a subterranean river to view in silence a cathedral-like dome studded with the tiny lights of thousands of glow-worms striving to attract minute insects to their sticky, prey-snaring "fishing lines".

The King Country was baptised by history. It was in the wilds of the region that the Maori King Tawhiao and his Kingite forces sought refuge after their attempts to block enforced European settlement had failed. To the Pakeha it was, for a generation, forbidden territory where the Maori King ruled as an independent monarch and strangers ventured at their peril. When an accommodation with the Government was finally achieved, the land was surveyed and formally granted to the tribes in possession of it. However, folklore persists of "secret understandings" with a succession of governments which preserved a degree of autonomy for several decades.

Since those stirring times much of the region has been opened for settlement, much land has been sold or leased and the Maori villages of Te Kuiti, Otorohanga and Taumarunui have grown into substantial towns. Yet a feeling of isolation persists, contributed to by some of the North Island's wildest country. A heavily dissected terrain is shrouded by virgin forest which conceals the true extent of its forbidding nature. After traversing the region the impression remains of a land disrupted but never mastered by human intrusion.

ISOLATION *The upper reaches of Kawhia Harbour harmonise with inland Waikato. The Kawhia area was the original homeland of the Ngati Toa warrior-chief, Te Rauparaha.*

TAHAROA IRONSANDS *The unusually pure sands are shipped to Japan for steel-making.*

Kawhia The long, languid reaches of an isolated harbour witnessed events that changed the pattern of the country's history. In 1821 Waikato tribes combined to attack Te Rauparaha and drive from the region the chief who was later to dominate much of the country. By the township is a vast and ageless pohutukawa tree to which the revered *Tainui* canoe, from which many tribes claim descent, is said to have been moored some 600 years ago. The canoe itself is said to be buried behind the Anaukiterangi meeting house close by where, according to tradition, stone slabs mark its bow and stern. To the south lie the pure ironsands of Taharoa, vast quantities of which are exported to Japan.

Ohakune Well patronised ski fields on the southern slopes of Mt Ruapehu, about 17 kilometres from the township, have accentuated the winter sports role of what had previously been a timber and market-gardening town spawned by the construction of the main-trunk railway. Après ski and hotel facilities are plentiful, but it is essential to book in advance.

Otorohanga This dairying centre draws travellers to its Kiwi House and Native Bird Centre, where native birds are bred.

Taumarunui Sited where the Ongarue River meets the Wanganui, the town serves an extensive farming and timber-producing district. It began as a Maori settlement on the junction of two important canoe routes. In summer, canoe parties leave here to paddle to the sea.

Te Kuiti The town combines farming, mining and milling, but is best known as a point from which to visit Waitomo. The splendid meeting house, built by Te Kooti's followers, was presented to the town in thanks for the sanctuary it afforded him at the end of the Land Wars.

Waitomo These world-famous limestone caves have long excited international admiration. Three caves have been developed for easy access and guided tours run regularly. The area has a vast labyrinth of systems, mostly uncharted, and one can only guess at what further wonders await discovery.

MT MESSENGER *Dense native bush and tree ferns characterise an area of unspoilt beauty.*

MOKAU RIVER ESTUARY *Limpid blue waters wind their way to the sea, with Egmont faint in the distance.*

NATIVE FLAX *Flowering stems stand tall.*

UMBRELLA FERN *One of six tree-fern species.*

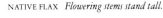

The dairy industry

The New Zealand dairy farmer ranks as the world's most efficient. For although the national dairy herd of about two million is only twelfth in size compared with those of other countries, New Zealand ranks as the foremost exporter of butter, cheese, milk powders and casein – and at the lowest prices.

Much of the credit for these achievements belongs to the industrious and enterprising dairy farmers and their capacity to organise, both individually and collectively. Their highly mechanised, one-person, "herring-bone" milking sheds can push cows through at the unbelievable rate of one per minute, and their co-operative dairy factories are envied the world over. However, the trigger to the blossoming of the industry lay in the application of artificial fertilisers. Dairy farmers were quick to exploit the possibilities afforded by the advent of refrigeration, but it was only at the turn of the century that the industry boomed to its present dominance.

Stock are not housed during the winter, and pasture provides most of their feed the year round. This gives local butter a high carotene content, making it much yellower than that produced in countries where cows are fed indoors for much of the year. But the feed requirements for a dairy farm are much more demanding than those for sheep. A herd is in milk for about ten months of the year, when feed needs are at their highest, whereas sheep can have their lambs sold at four months and so be off a property before feed becomes scarce either from a dry summer or from a prolonged winter. Thus the country's dairy farms are concentrated overwhelmingly in the North Island, and generally in the rich, fertile lowlands to the north and west where summer rainfall is high and the winters short. Well-drained soils there can stand up to trampling by cattle, and in such a setting the relative economics of dairying and sheep-farming usually enable dairy farmers to outbid their competitors for available land.

The general pattern is slightly modified by those who supply town milk. Here, the whole herd may not be able to be "dried off" for the winter (by timing their calving for the spring) and a greater degree of feeding-out is necessary.

Almost all dairy produce is manufactured in co-operative factories owned and managed by the dairy farmers. Many of these are world leaders in the technology of milk processing. Ubiquitous milk tankers call to collect milk and cream from the farm gate and trundle it to the factories for processing into butter, cheese, casein or milk powder. The factories pay the farmer on the basis of the weight of the butterfat supplied, and the performance of each herd is carefully monitored. The resulting products are marketed by a central body, the New Zealand Dairy Board, whose sales-people scour the world for export markets and whose consulting officers advise on herd improvement, test each herd and run an artificial breeding centre.

The Bay of Plenty

MOUNT MAUNGANUI VIEWED FROM THE MOUNT *Seen from the summit of the volcanic cone is the low sand bar that built up gradually until finally tying the cone to the mainland and the busy port it now houses. The sands of Ocean Beach stretch away into the distance.*

"Tickle the soil with a hoe, and it will laugh a harvest" – if propagandists often oversold the attractions of new lands to would-be migrants, this area is one which has fully met the most extravagant claims. Indeed, its first European visitor, Captain Cook, extolled the region's "plenty" after experiencing apparent "poverty" on the neighbouring East Cape. Here much of the country's prized kiwifruit and tamarillos is harvested. Here the logs of sprawling forests of *radiata* pine are converted into pulp and paper, or shipped out from Mount Maunganui as logs. Here tens of thousands flock each Christmas-time, to double the population and savour long, sun-drenched beaches and the thrill of big-game fishing. Here, too, many choose a warm and friendly place to which to retire.

INTO THE SURF *The Ocean Beach at Mount Maunganui is a favourite with surfers. In the distance lies Mayor Island, popular as a base for the big-game fishermen who come to the Bay of Plenty each year.*

East Cape Road The stretch of coastline that lies between Opotiki and Gisborne provides some of the finest seascapes in the country. A seemingly endless series of nooks and crannies is spiced with an eventful past which reflects several of the key phases in the country's development, from the coming of the Polynesian to Captain Cook and the whalers who followed him.

It was at Whangaparaoa (the Bay of Whales) that two of the revered ancestral canoes are said to have first landed, the *Tainui* and the *Arawa.* They arrived so close to each other in time and place as to dispute the ownership of a whale beached here. This gives rise to the possibility that the two canoes may have travelled from "Hawaiki" (the Maori's legendary homeland) as a double-hulled canoe, dividing to make a safe landfall. Here, too, the wife of the captain of the *Tainui* is said to have made the first plant-

GATE PA *St George's Church at Gate Pa, on the approach to Tauranga, records the events of 29 April 1864 when British troops endeavoured unsuccessfully to dislodge followers of the Maori King from a fortified pa. It had been constructed as a challenge to troops stationed at Tauranga attempting to block communication between Kingite followers on the East Cape with those fighting in the Waikato. Two earlier pa had been built farther away, and the Kingites had even formed a road in from the coast to one of them "so that the soldiers will not be too tired to fight" when the British launched their assault. Twice their chief had written to the British general, informing him of the pa and of the road built for his use, but silence had followed these knightly challenges as the British were waiting for reinforcements. In the meantime the Kingites moved here, building their third pa by a gate in a post-and-rail fence dividing Maori from European-owned land (on the site of today's memorial church). When the attack came, some 1,650 troops were pitted against barely 250 defenders, and were supported in the assault by a variety of heavy artillery, which pounded the pa. The defenders attempted to withdraw, but fire from the rear forced them back into the pa where they inflicted heavy casualties on soldiers bewildered by the maze of fortifications. One third of the storming party fell, including a colonel and most of the officers, for only about 25 Kingite casualties. The chivalry displayed by the Kingites throughout the day was remarkable. After a subsequent clash at Te Ranga, in which the Kingites were soundly defeated, an unusual "Order for the Day" was discovered in which the Kingite warriors were enjoined to exercise the highest level of gallantry.*

ings of kumara, the sweet potato whose introduction led to a remarkable change in the Maori way of life. The kumara was once seen as dividing the Archaic from the Classic Maori culture, but it is now clear that the two phases overlapped, with the impact of horticulture spread over several centuries.

Cape Runaway, the eastern extremity of the Bay of Plenty, was named by Captain Cook in 1769 as he journeyed from Poverty Bay after his initial unhappy landing at Gisborne, en route to the Coromandel Peninsula where he was to claim the land for the British Crown. A group of intrepid Maori had put out from the shore to investigate the interloper, but Cook "at this time being very busy" could not afford the time to watch them. Grapeshot was fired towards but not at them, and the warriors, who could never in their lives have experienced anything like it before, prudently paddled furiously away.

Te Kaha, a delightful cove, has the earthworks of a pa which witnessed many

HOLIDAY MAKERS SAVOUR THE SUN *Large numbers of visitors come to enjoy the region's long, hot summers and its welcoming beaches.*

IN MEMORIAM Otemataha Pa Military Cemetery, in Tauranga, holds many of the dead from the engagements at Gate Pa and Te Ranga. Among those buried was Col. H. J. P. Booth, who won the unenviable distinction of being the most senior officer to be killed in the Land Wars. Here, on the headstone of a chief who fell at Te Ranga, a Kingite is portrayed carrying water to British wounded in one of a series of acts of high chivalry witnessed in action at Gate Pa.

THE MONMOUTH REDOUBT *Trenches were dug by British troops in 1864 to guard Tauranga from tribes who were resisting enforced land sales. Several of the redoubt's guns are still here.*

battles in pre-European times, including a sustained seige in 1834. Relics of the bay whalers who operated around the Cape are also to be seen, both at Te Kaha and at Raukokore, where the Catholic Church has a venerable whalebone arch.

Katikati The small rural community in the lee of the rugged Kaimai Ranges enjoys the warmth of both the climate and the hot mineral springs close by. The settlement began in the aftermath of the Land Wars, when the Government was fostering European immigration in the belief that only a strong European population in the North Island could secure the peace. Free passages were offered, with larger grants of land for those who contributed to their own fares. Between 1871 and 1880 more than 100,000 assisted immigrants arrived. Against this background, the Orangeman George Veysey Stewart organised the largest single migration of Irish, 4,000 of whom came to Katikati under the promise of a living easily won from the most fertile of soils. Hitherto, comparatively few Irish had migrated to New Zealand.

Kawerau Situated on level land in the Tarawera River's central valley is one of the country's most industrialised towns, developed as a centre for the processing of forest products. The pulp-and-paper mill site was chosen because of the presence of geothermal steam, which is used in the processes. Tours over the mill are given each afternoon. The town's name, taken from the locality, commemorates a grandson of Toi, the legendary figure who inhabited Whakatane.

Maketu A coastal settlement with two interesting carved meeting houses. Maketu (named for a place in Hawaiki, the Maori's legendary homeland) was where the much revered *Arawa* canoe, from which Rotorua's Arawa people trace their descent, made its final landfall.

Mayor Island Named (with the Alderman Islands to the north-west) by Captain Cook in a moment of frivolity almost wholly lacking in his choice of place-names. The island, resting invitingly some 30 kilometres offshore, is set in waters that teem with such big-game fish as marlin, tuna, kingfish and shark. A number of world records have been set here. The season for the larger fish extends from mid-December to May, but its popularity is such as to make advance booking essential. For those who prefer land to water, tracks lead through delightful bush to pa sites and to the lakes in the twin volcanic craters. Trips can be arranged from Tauranga, Mount Mau-

nganui, Whakatane and Whangamata. There is also good skin-diving to be had around the pohutukawa-fringed coastline.

Mount Maunganui Dominated by the cone of "the Mount", Mount Maunganui was for many years little more than a restful seaside settlement before the maturing of the vast pine forests nearby compelled its development as a deep-water port. The Mount affords a magnificent panorama to those who make the climb (1½ hrs return). Inevitably, once the site of a huge fortified pa, the Mount was the scene of an epic battle about 200 years ago. At its foot is a naturally heated salt-water swimming pool and on the famous sweep of Ocean Beach is the blowhole of Leisure Island.

"THE ELMS" *Tauranga grew up around this elegant mission house (1838–47), built by Archdeacon A. N. Brown. The mission was not a success and closed when military settlers took over the district.*

MIDDEN AT THE MOUNT *A pile of shells, the legacy of an ancient feast, at the base of the Mount. Middens such as these assist archaeologists in their study of occupation sites. Fortunately Prehistoric Man was as untidy as his modern counterpart and many "picnic" sites have been identified.*

POHATUROA ROCK *Once a tohunga's cave, now Whakatane's war memorial. The canoe is the* Mataatua.

RIDING THE RAPIDS *Finding adventure on the Wairoa River.*

Ohope A good beach renders Ohope a deservedly popular summer holiday spot. Augmenting the appeal of the open sea are the sheltered waters of Ohiwa Harbour, severed from the ocean by a slim peninsula and affording excellent fishing and water-skiing. Wainui, at the head of the harbour, was where the redoubtable Te Kooti was granted an area of land for himself and his relatives following his pardon in 1883 for his leadership of the last of the armed uprisings against European settlement in the country. No one knows where the old warrior was finally laid to rest, but it is believed to be in this vicinity.

Opotiki The tranquil dairying and fruit-growing town, now the commercial centre of the south-eastern Bay of Plenty, witnessed extraordinary scenes a century ago. European settlement dates from 1865, when a military garrison was established in the aftermath of the gruesome murder of the Rev. Carl Volkner, the local missionary remembered at the Church of St Stephen the Martyr.

Te Puke Much of the country's kiwifruit, and a quarter of its citrus fruit, is produced in this astonishingly fertile district. The kiwifruit harvest is celebrated in May. The township was first settled towards the end of the nineteenth century.

Te Ranga Pa A short distance from Tauranga, in Pyes Pa Road, are the remnants of the pa where the British troops exacted a terrible vengeance for their defeat at Gate Pa.

1. *The Kawerau Mill and Mt Edgecumbe. The model town of Kawerau was built in 1953 when a giant pulp-and-paper mill was erected to process neighbouring stands of pine. Here some of the world's fastest newsprint machines produce hundreds of thousands of tonnes of newsprint each year, much for export to Australia and beyond.* 2. *Cut logs are also shipped out through the port at Mount Maunganui.* 2.

A MISSIONARY "MARTYR" The Church of St Stephen the Martyr, Opotiki, records a tragedy unique in New Zealand, for here a missionary, the Rev. Carl Volkner, was martyred in 1865, and his blood served in the chalice in a macabre parody of the Last Supper. Volkner died at the hands of the Hauhau, a movement that saw the Maori as betrayed by the missionaries who had once seemed to support them (Bishop Selwyn had unwisely chosen to serve as chaplain to the British troops). Many Maori had readily embraced Christianity as a religion of peace after inter-tribal wars with newly gained guns had inflicted enormous casualties. Now seemingly denied by the God they had worshipped, the Hauhau developed a creed which equated the Maori with the Israelites in Egypt and in less sanguinary ceremonies intoned chants to induce the Pakeha to leave the country. Volkner's headstone is in the east wall.

WAIOEKA SCENIC HIGHWAY *The landscape on the direct route between Gisborne and Opotiki, dramatic though it is, is surpassed by that of the slower East Cape road, especially at Christmas, when flowering pohutukawa spike the seascapes. The two routes make a most satisfying round trip.*

Whakatane Characterising the town is the sheer rock of Pohaturoa, which rises oddly from its commercial heart. In tradition, the rock provided a tohunga with a cave. In its shadow, local chiefs signed the Treaty of Waitangi. The town is the centre of a rich dairying and fat-lamb producing region, rich also in timber from the nearby expanses of the Kaingaroa Forest. Inland lies the native bush of the Urewera National Park (*q.v.*), reached only on foot from this aspect. By the rock is a model of the fabled *Mataatua* canoe, to whose crew local tribes trace their ancestry. The canoe's arrival gave the locality its name (literally, to act as a man). A woman, Wairaka, prevented the newly arrived canoe from drifting out to sea by seizing a paddle and, with a cry of "Kia whakatane au i ahau!" (I will act as a man!), averted tragedy. Her statue stands on a rock at Whakatane Heads.

White Island Some 50 kilometres offshore from Whakatane billows the country's only marine volcano, whose links with the activity in the Rotorua and Taupo areas can be seen from the air on a clear day. The island has occasionally been mined for sulphur. Twelve people are known to have died as the result of its unpredictable activity and today it is given over to birds and derelict mining buildings.

CARAVANS AND CANVAS *Summer at the Mount Maunganui motor camp.*

Tauranga The city of Tauranga spreads pleasantly round the southernmost tip of a large natural harbour, facing across the water to Mount Maunganui and the Pacific Ocean. "The Mount" boasts a magnificent deep-water harbour, thanks to extensive dredging, and commercial life divides between the two centres. Surrounding the city are prolific orcharding areas, thick with the lush growth of subtropical fruits which reflect the warmth of the climate and the mildness of the winters. The burgeoning of both the city and the port is comparatively recent, dating from the post-war maturing of vast pine forests and the development of both a pulp-and-paper industry and an export trade in sawn logs. This was followed in 1976 by the completion of the Kaimai Tunnel, which diverts to Mount Maunganui produce from the Waikato that would otherwise have passed through Auckland, and has confirmed Tauranga's shipping role as the country's largest port by volume of cargo.

Within the city's limits are picturesque reminders of its beginnings. A pretty but substantial mission house marks the spot where European settlement began with the labours of a single diligent missionary; ominous earthworks remain from the redoubt built by the British troops who followed to displace the gospel with the gun; nearby, the dead from Gate Pa and Te Ranga lie in the tiny Otemataha Pa Military Cemetery, slaughtered in battle and buried by the grief-stricken cleric. In no other New Zealand city are the origins of settlement as well preserved, perhaps because growth came late and only after public attitudes to relics of the past had changed from indifference to dedication.

Also recalling the past is Tauranga Historic Village, a living recreation of Victorian times with an emphasis on the district's military background and serving as a focal point for specialist hobby groups. The ocean and harbour beaches are complemented by natural hot pools at Welcome Bay and Plummers Point, and in Cambridge Road. There are pleasant walks to Kaiate Falls, McLaren Falls and along the Ohauiti walkway.

Maori arts and crafts

Over centuries of isolation, a vigorous and highly distinctive style of art was evolved by the New Zealand Maori.

The complex geometric patterns of woven work — traditionally undertaken by women — contrast with the sweeping curvilinear forms of carving, the work of men. While the women plaited mats and baskets from flax, or wove cloaks decorated with feathers or dogskin and brightly coloured, geometric *taniko* borders, the men carved. They carved anything that was carvable — even themselves, etching into their flesh the deep blue-black tattoo lines of the *moko*.

But it was in woodcarving that Maori art reached its most fantastic accomplishments. The Maori constructed houses, fortifications and war canoes, and wrought weapons, ornaments, utensils and musical instruments. They decorated them with a profusion of figures and designs. On treasure boxes, house carvings and canoes, stylised figures with protruding tongues and glaring eyes of iridescent paua shell writhe between *manaia*, birdlike monsters whose forms are entangled with interlocking spirals of almost filigree delicacy. By contrast, the inside walls of tribal meeting houses are lined with ancestor figures which are carved with massive boldness and solidity to support the roof rafters painted in rhythmic, colourful patterns called *kowhaiwhai*.

Greenstone ornaments were necessarily less intricate. Working only with water, sandstone and sometimes generations of patience, the Maori produced weapons and ornaments such as the well-known *hei-tiki* from translucent nephrite and bowenite. Their clean, simple lines belie the care of their manufacture and the value attached to them.

New Zealand's museums are well stocked with examples of Maori art, but they are not echoes of a dead culture. Only a few elderly women still bear the *moko*, but the other arts and crafts of the Maori are thriving. At the Maori Arts and Crafts Institute, Whakarewarewa (see p. 63), one can watch artists at work and apprentices in training, and purchase examples of their skill. The government sponsors other training programmes, while many individual exponents of carving and weaving continue to work and teach in the traditional manner. New carvings are made not only for marae and meeting houses, but also for universities, government buildings and churches. Flax baskets are a common sight, though today they are likely to carry groceries or school books.

Unique in itself, Maori art highlights New Zealand's uniqueness in the world. It is no coincidence that the huge jets of the national airline, as far removed from classical Maori technology as stone tools are from our own, carry as their logo the traditional symbol of the *koru*.

MAORI CENTENNIAL MEMORIAL MEETING HOUSE, WAITANGI (1940) *This uniquely carved* whare runanga *contains superb examples of carving from throughout the North Island.*

The East Cape and Gisborne

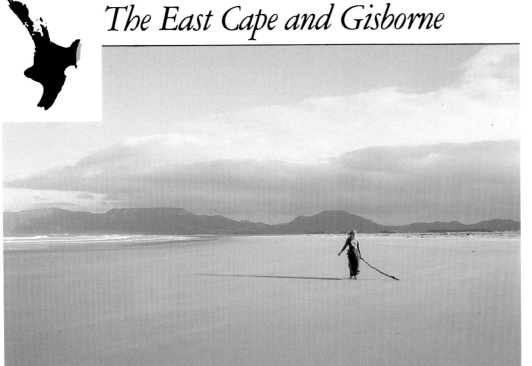

Kaiti Hill lookout and Poho-o-rawiri meeting house deserve a visit.

Hicks Bay Points of interest include a splendid carved meeting house, picturesque Horseshoe Bay, good sea fishing, a bush walk to glow-worms, and a derelict freezing works – one of several that closed when roads came to the Cape. It is a popular camping place.

Manutuke A finely carved meeting house incorporates two major Maori legends – the tearing apart of the Sky Father from the Earth Mother, and the fishing up by Maui of the North Island from the sea.

Matawhero The Presbyterian Church, the oldest in Poverty Bay, dates from 1862, and was the only building in the area to be spared by Te Kooti in his campaign against the local settlers.

Patutahi Close by is Rongopai meeting house, built for Te Kooti and decorated with exuberant wall paintings.

Ruatoria Principal centre of the Ngati Porou, where on occasions important tribal ceremonies take place at the Mangahanea marae. Mt Hikurangi (1,839 m) stands due west and is reputed to be the first point on earth to be touched by the new day's sun.

Te Araroa On the foreshore, near "the world's most easterly hotel", stands a massive and venerable pohutukawa (*pictured*). From here a road leads to the lighthouse on the tip of East Cape.

Te Puia The small settlement of Te Puia, with its trees and tiny lake, is a welcome contrast to the rather barren countryside. There is evidence of thermal activity, with a warm, open mineral pool and hot mineral baths at the motel.

Tikitiki The elaborate interior of St Mary's Maori Church (*pictured*) contrasts sharply with its simple exterior.

Tokomaru Bay The locality reflects the vital role that shipping once enjoyed around the Cape, then its only lifeline to the outside world.

TE ARAROA BEACH *Exhilarating, deserted sweeps of golden sand are a feature of the Cape. In such a setting it is hard to conjure images of the past, when wool was ferried out to ships in surfboats, and sheep, cattle and horses brought in. Timber was simply thrown overboard to be swept ashore by the tide.*

The East Cape's attractions are more real than simply "the world's most easterly hotel" and a mountain, Hikurangi, whose summit first sees a new day's sun. For the Cape was a beginning. Tradition holds that several of the migratory canoes from Hawaiki first touched here, and it was at Gisborne that members of Captain Cook's expedition became the first Europeans to land in New Zealand.

The atmosphere of origins still lingers. Inland, the brooding primeval forest of the Ureweras; venerable, venerated carved meeting houses, and land still suffering from misuse by early European leaseholders (much still Maori-owned), contribute to an overall sense of remoteness. Yet for many this is merely background to a sun-drenched cape studded with inviting beaches, for which the Maori "Christmas tree", the flame-flowered pohutukawa whose gnarled roots seem impervious to salt water, are a common backdrop.

Anaura Bay A classic, lonely beach, this was where Cook made a second landing in search of supplies after his bloody encounter at Gisborne.

Gisborne Fertile market gardens set in verdant valleys surround the city and today mock Cook's name for the area, Poverty Bay. Despite its remoteness, events here changed the course of history: Cook's first landing-place was Kaiti Beach, and it was a local Maori, Te Kooti, who led a brilliant campaign of Maori resistance in the Land Wars with the settlers. Both are remembered in a variety of ways. The beaches here, and some of the country's warmest weather, assure an annual invasion of summertime sunseekers. The museum and art gallery,

TE ARAROA'S CHRISTMAS TREE *New Zealand's most massive pohutukawa.*

CAPTAIN JAMES COOK Dour Yorkshireman and navigator extraordinary, Captain James Cook (1728–79) sailed under secret sealed instructions to seek the land Tasman had seen in 1642. Cook first made landfall on 9 October 1769, but, as with Tasman before him, the local tribe felt threatened and, after bloodshed on Gisborne's Kaiti Beach, a sorrowing Cook departed, naming the area "Poverty Bay", for it afforded him nothing he wanted. Sailing north, he first landed at Anaura Bay and was then directed to Cooks Cove, near Tolaga Bay, where he replenished his supplies and marvelled at the natural archway.

A MAORI MEMORIAL *St Mary's Church, Tikitiki, was built as a memorial to Ngati Porou servicemen killed in the 1914–1918 war, two of whom are depicted in the east window.*

MORERE HOT SPRINGS Nestled enticingly in a bush reserve studded with groves of statuesque nikau are the inviting Morere hot thermal springs, their waters tinged with iodine and lent added curative properties by calcium and sodium chloride. The springs are isolated, being well east of the volcanic belt. Morere, whose name means "a swing" or "a giant's stride", is an ideal stopping place for a picnic and a swim.

Tolaga Bay A sheep-farming centre by the Uawa river mouth, the settlement has a good beach and is close by Cooks Cove, where a relieved Cook found an hospitable welcome.

Waioeka scenic highway Attractive though this slick, direct route between Gisborne and Opotiki may be, the traveller with time to spare should opt for the longer, more leisurely coastal road.

Waihau (Loisels) Beach A typical crescent of golden sand.

Waipiro Bay Once the largest settlement on the East Cape, the township all but died with the demise of coastal shipping and the bypassing of the main road.

Whangaparaoa Famed in tradition, it was here that the *Arawa* and the *Tainui*, two of the fabled canoes of the so-called "Great Migration", landed – so close in time as to argue over ownership of a stranded whale. Folklore also has it that this area saw the introduction of the kumara, which was eventually to transform the Maori economy from that of roving hunter-gatherer to settled agriculturalist.

EAST CAPE LIGHTHOUSE *The light marks the mainland's most easterly point, perceptively identified as such by Cook though he had scarcely begun to circumnavigate the island. East Island, just offshore, was originally home to the light but proved too inhospitable, four men drowning whilst landing supplies.*

Urewera National Park

A GRAND WILDERNESS *The Urewera National Park offers the most spectacular and remote tramping in the North Island.*

TE WHAI-A-TE-MOTU (1870–88) *The meeting house of Mataatua, near Ruatahuna.*

CASCADING WATER *The park boasts many small but spectacular falls.*

The vast brooding forest of the Urewera evokes powerful imagery. Here in mythology a taniwha gouged the lake from the ranges in a frantic attempt to reach the sea; here since antiquity have lived the Tuhoe, the "children of the mist"; here more recently the colonial government stalked Te Kooti in the closing stages of the Land Wars. Despite the coming of the road, one can still feel in this majestic setting the apartness that at the turn of the century saw local Tuhoe deny the Governor entry and permit the Premier to visit their revered meeting house at Mataatua only after he had surrendered his knife, pipe and tobacco.

The national park, with headquarters at Aniwaniwa, centres on the 55 square kilometres of Lake Waikaremoana, a lake whose fabled fishing is rivalled by the tramping and hunting to be had in the surrounding forest.

2.

3.

THE CATCH *Lake Waikaremoana yields one of its plentiful rainbow trout.*

IMAGES OF UREWERA 1. *Camping area, Mokau* 2. *Old timber wagon* 3. *Dracophyllum, a distinctive bush feature.*

WAIKAREITI *Surrounded by primeval bush and reached only by walking track, the lake contains six small islands. One, Rahui, contains its own lakelet. Inaccessibility renders the area a botanists' paradise.*

Surrounding Lake Waikaremoana is a belt of northern rata, rimu and tawa forest, with some miro, hinau and tawhero. Above the level of the lake, red and silver beech gradually assume dominance until at about 1,200 metres the red beech disappears and stands of pure silver beech continue to the timberline. Kiwi, kaka and most other native birds are found throughout.

The ancient Maori had little impact on the environment here; tracks and small eel weirs caused little disturbance. They were also careful to avoid polluting water.

With the Pakeha came problems at Waikaremoana and a decision to end hotel accommodation at Lake House, thus moving habitation away from the lake to reduce enrichment of its waters. Today, however, an excellent camping ground, with cabins and first-class chalet accommodation, allows visitors the luxury of an extended stay at Waikaremoana – "sea of rippling waters".

"CHILD OF THE MIST" *A Tuhoe youngster.*

TRAMPERS *One of the gentler walks.*

KAKABEAK *Distinctive bush blossoms.*

RUA KENANA (1867–1935) He set up a community at Maungapohatu and to his followers he was a prophet. To others, including the government, he was a subversive and a charlatan. Colourful, enigmatic, he is still revered by some, despite prosecution and jail.

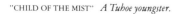

Hawke's Bay

"THE SPIRIT OF NAPIER" *A landmark on Napier's Marine Parade.*

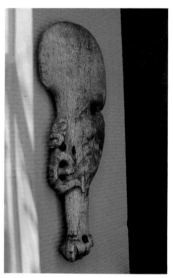

BLOODSTAINED PATU *A gruesome whale-bone museum exhibit from the 1860s.*

THE GREEN GRASS OF THE BAY *Hawke's Bay's pastures, here pictured in the flush of growth, can in the height of summer be bleached grey-white by weeks of unremitting sunshine.*

"TOILERS OF THE SEA" *Alan Strathern's sculpture at Napier's aquarium.*

TOWERING PALMS *Napier's Kennedy Road imparts an unusually tropical air.*

NAPIER'S AQUARIUM *A multitude of smaller fish to offset the more dynamic display at nearby Marineland.*

WOOL FOR WEAVING *Lambs are reared especially to provide weavers and spinners with a variety of wools.*

A broad sweep of coastline embraces some of the country's finest areas for sheep rearing, orcharding and market gardening as well as the world's only known mainland colony of gannets.

The region pivots on the twin cities of Napier and Hastings, of nearly identical population but radically different in topography and purpose. Napier spills down a sheer bluff to her port and a tree-lined Marine Parade crammed with every form of entertainment. Hastings, as level as a city can be, is ringed with orchards and houses huge food-processing factories, but has less obvious claims for the visitor's attention. For a time Hastings seemed destined to dominate her sister, but the massive earthquake which in 1931 all but destroyed both centres, was creative as well as destructive – large areas of land beside Napier were raised from below sea level to provide it with critically needed space for growth. Despite some intensely fertile alluvial coastal areas, the coastline is in the main both rocky and precipitous. Inland the hills build into rugged ranges which produce a "rain shadow" effect, giving Hawke's Bay both a low rainfall and high sunshine.

FOOD PROCESSING *Hastings produces much of the country's canned and frozen food. Plantings are staggered so that in the harvest season both the food-processing factories and the gangs in the fields can work round the clock to pick the crop at its peak. There is a high demand for seasonal labour.*

Dannevirke and Norsewood Both towns were originally settled by Scandinavians who came to cut a road through the dense forests that once cloaked southern Hawke's Bay. Dannevirke has blossomed into a bustling farming centre, while Norsewood maintains a quieter pace, its origins reflected in a nostalgic museum.

Hastings The city lies long and low on the lengthy Heretaunga Plains, a flatness broken only by the hills of nearby Havelock North, its most desirable "suburb". The plains produce vast quantities of fruit and vegetables to feed the city's huge food-processing factories for canning and quick-freezing. Especially rich and intensively farmed are areas around the Ngaruroro, Tutaekuri and Tukituki Rivers. Highland Games each Easter draw visitors from far and wide, although its high temperatures and relative proximity to East Coast beaches make Hastings a popular summer resort as well. Fantasyland excites children the year round.

HAWKE BAY *The bay itself, with the hump of Napier's Bluff Hill in the distance.*

PANIA OF THE REEF *Napier's love-forlorn maiden.*

SHOW JUMPING *Equestrian sports, including polo, have a strong following in the Hawke's Bay district.*

Napier Curious Bluff Hill, originally an island but now tied to the land by a sand bar, gives Napier an unusual identity, accentuated by a Marine Parade which deliberately and unselfconsciously claims the role of a seaside holiday centre. There among lines of Norfolk pines await a remarkable Marineland, an excellent aquarium, a kiwi display house and a wide variety of games and amusements. So, too, does the statue of Pania, a mermaid who in legend came ashore and fell in love with a local warrior but who, when she swam back to see her people, was dragged down to an underwater reef where she may still be seen, her hair flowing like seaweed from the rock.

The city is not only the region's port but is also the country's largest wool centre, with millions of dollars of wool changing hands – mostly to foreign buyers – at regular auctions. In 1931 the city was flattened in the greatest natural disaster the country has known. The trail of destruction stretched the length of Hawke's Bay: huge sections of coastline slumped into the sea, rivers changed course, bridges buckled and vast cracks opened all over the countryside. The city was left in ruins. In all, some 256 were killed; the material loss was incalculable.

Lake Tutira The pretty bird sanctuary recalls the author-naturalist who described breaking in the land here as "a compromise between murdering the sheep and 'making' the country".

Waipawa and Waipukurau Significant farming centres in central Hawke's Bay. Above Waipukurau's main street are the remains of the pa beside which the town grew up.

Wairoa Northern Hawke's Bay's only substantial centre, Wairoa is set in dairying and sheep- and cattle-raising country. Nearby is the beautiful Mahia Peninsula which marks the region's northern boundary.

NAPIER'S MARINELAND Here, dolphins, seals and other mammals delight with breathtaking displays of speed, intelligence and ingenuity.

CAPE KIDNAPPERS Looking towards Cape Kidnappers (*above*), and two of the thousands of gannets which congregate there from about July to April each year (*below*). The Cape, best visited on foot from Clifton (eight kilometres return), was named by Captain Cook in 1769 after local Maoris attempted to make off with a Polynesian servant boy. The *Endeavour's* cannons fired, confusion reigned, and the boy dived from his kidnappers' canoe and swam back to the ship. In the excitement, no one seemed to notice the world's only known mainland gannetry.

"SCANDY" WHEELS *One of several exhibits in Norsewood's museum which recall the area's links with its Scandinavian pioneers.*

WINE

The New Zealand wine industry, after suffering from decades of official neglect and little public demand, has blossomed in recent years. After the budget in 1958 slashed wine imports, the country's winemakers expanded their vineyards and increased their plantings of classic varieties. Since then, too, the public palate has been sharpened. Consumption has also been boosted by New Zealanders' propensity to travel to Europe (where a taste for wine is an almost obligatory requirement), as well as by the success of local wines (particularly whites) in international wine fairs. As a result, New Zealanders are now drinking more wine per head than ever before, with local wines claiming most of the market. The major commercial vineyards are to be found in Hawke's Bay and around Hen-

derson (near Auckland) and Blenheim.

The origins of New Zealand's wine industry are obscure. The grape was introduced by the first missionary, Samuel Marsden, in 1819, and the British Resident at Waitangi was producing wine in the 1830s. The first act on the part of the French settlers at Akaroa, too, was to establish small vineyards. However, the oldest winery in the country, dating from 1865, is in Hawke's Bay, at Greenmeadows, where a Catholic Mission still produces sacramental wine but has broadened as well into the secular market. All the wineries welcome visitors, both to taste and to buy, and some arrange conducted tours of their establishments. Among those worth visiting in Hawke's Bay are the Mission, Vidals, Glenvale and Te Mata estates.

ASPECTS OF THE REGION'S WINE INDUSTRY *Grapes being harvested in Havelock North vineyards (1 & 2); wine ageing in oak casks (3); grapes ripening in the Mission Vineyard at Greenmeadows (4); the monastery at Greenmeadows which began winemaking to supply the needs of those performing Mass (5).*

BLUE PENGUINS *Common around the Hawke's Bay coast, the penguin is evenly feathered, with wings reduced to flippers.*

MAIN STREET LIGHT *Wairoa's lighthouse, moved to its present site near the river from an offshore island, is lit each evening.*

Thermal activity

Hot springs are found in many parts of the world, generally in regions of faulted and folded rocks and particularly in areas of recent or continuing volcanic activity. Just occasionally, hot springs contain boiling water, either from cold water which has struck hot rocks or from water which has been trapped temporarily under thick mud.

Geysers form near rivers or lakes, where water seeps down deep channels far into the earth. When it strikes hot rock, steam begins to form, forcing progressively more water up and out of the column, and creating more and more steam. The column gradually becomes lighter and suddenly, as the last of the water is forced upwards, a steam explosion occurs, spouting water high into the air. Where more hot water can then flow into the column, eruptions can continue for some time, as with Whakarewarewa's Pohutu geyser. After an eruption the water settles, the channel gradually fills once more and the process is repeated. The channel itself is generally broken into sharp bends, which effectively prevent convection and so stop the water from mixing to a uniform temperature. Where convection can occur, instead of the water becoming superheated and exploding, thermal pools are formed. The boiling waters also contain dissolved minerals, which slowly build into curious and often colourful silica formations as water evaporates on the surface. No one can predict when a particular geyser will erupt: some do several times an hour; some not for days, or even weeks. They are, however, most active when barometric pressures are low, as this reduces the downward pressure of the column and can precipitate activity.

There are only three noted groups of geysers in the world – in New Zealand, at Rotorua; in Iceland ("the land of frost and fire") and in the United States' Yellowstone Park.

New Zealand's active volcanoes are confined to the Taupo Volcanic Belt, a chain which reaches from the peaks of the Tongariro National Park to where White Island belches steam into the Bay of Plenty sky. Similarly, the largest and hottest of the country's thermal springs are found in this zone. Activity is seen at its most spectacular in a number of valleys near Rotorua and Taupo, and is tapped for the generation of electricity at Wairakei.

To win steam for power generation, bores are sunk and cased with tubes. The escaping steam is then "dried" and led to low-pressure turbines. Water taken from the Waikato River is used to condense the steam as it leaves the turbines, causing it to contract and create a vacuum. This helps double the turbines' output from what it would have been had the steam simply been released into the atmosphere. So far drilling here has only begun to tap the area's potential, and there are plans to increace greatly the amount of electricity generated in this way.

The thermal region

TUDOR TOWERS *Rotorua's old bath house.*   BELLBIRD *A honey-eater best heard at dawn.*

For over a century Rotorua has held irresistible fascination, with geysers, boiling mud, furious fumeroles and warm mineral bathing pools as well as myriad lakes, well-rewarded trout fishing and a substratum of Maori culture. This last is commercialised as nowhere else, assuring a wide range of Maori arts and crafts and rousing Maori concerts.

The city skirts the southern shore of Lake Rotorua, serving both as the region's principal commercial centre and the North Island's premier tourist resort. Much of the surrounding land is given over to extensive forestry and sheep farming, introduced to resettle servicemen returning from the 1939–45 war. Despite these substantial preoccupations, for the visitor the lingering impressions are of warm earth, of steam percolating through the most unlikely crevices – from under gravestones and out of street drains – and of an ever-present, pungent odour of hydrogen sulphide.

In mythology, thermal activity came in answer to the prayers of a chief as he lay freezing on a mountaintop; in legend, this was the setting for the romance between Hinemoa and Tutanekai; and in history it was here that Hongi Hika brought his canoes to attack Mokoia Island.

LORD OF THE GEYSERS *Whakarewarewa's massive Pohutu regularly plays to heights in excess of 30 metres.*

TARAWERA LAKE AND MOUNTAIN *A phantom canoe seen on the lake in 1886 was regarded as a premonition of the mountain's eruption only eleven days later.*

"THE WHITE TERRACES, ROTOMAHANA" *A painting by Charles Blomfield before the 1886 eruption.* Auckland City Art Gallery

RAINBOW SPRINGS Unique trout springs offer bush walks and the opportunity to feed brown and rainbow trout.

COLONIAL VILLAGE *A place to browse.*

VINTAGE "INDIAN" *A lovingly maintained motorcycle ready to rally.*

1.

2.

3.

MONEY FOR JAM *A young "pennydiver" at Whakarewarewa.*

A sample of the scenes that await at Whakarewarewa, on the outskirts of Rotorua. 1. Apprentice carvers at work at the Maori Arts and Craft Institute, where master carvers pass on their ever more appreciated skills to the next generation. Straight-grained kauri and totara are favoured woods. Traditionally carving was amongst the most venerated of callings: women were not permitted even to be present, and waste chips were carefully collected to prevent them being used in cooking fires. 2. Bizarre pools of boiling mud. 3. A concert party performs an action song. Maori "traditional dress" is less revealing than in pre-missionary times, when men often went naked and women, when not wearing a cloak, covered only their waists. 4. A carved gatepost at the entrance of the Model Village, depicting the lovers Hinemoa and Tutanekai. 5. A flax weaver at the Institute introduces visitors to her craft. Flax was put to a wide variety of uses, providing fibre for making garments, mats, fishing lines and ropes. Green leaves were used to weave baskets, eel-pots and nets. The fibre is obtained by soaking the leaves in water and then scraping off the unwanted tissue. 6. Cooking in thermal steam. The Maori's main way of cooking was by steaming food in earth ovens. A hole was dug and lined with red-hot stones. These were covered with green vegetation, the food was placed on top and the whole oven splashed with water and sealed with more vegetation and earth. Here at Whakarewarewa natural steam made cooking much simpler!

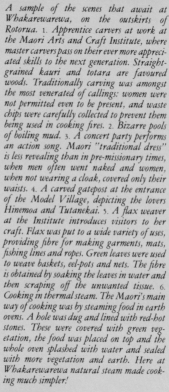

4.

5.

6.

WHAKAREWAREWA *A general view of the eerie scene which draws visitors from all parts of the world.*

A BROODING, AWESOME VALLEY *Waimangu lacks Whaka's fury but more than compensates in atmosphere.*

NEAR WAIOTAPU *There are many hot streams in the region, where locals go to bathe.*

Blue and Green Lakes In favourable light there is an astonishing difference in the appearance of the two lakes, despite their being the closest of neighbours. Although well able to be appreciated from the roadside, the lakes are perhaps best seen from the track that runs along the shoulder that separates them. The lakes lie by the road to Te Wairoa Buried Village and Lake Tarawera.

Lake Okataina Of the many lakes in the region, Okataina is arguably the most enchanting, completely encircled by native bush and with a magical approach along a road canopied by native fuchsia. Sandy beaches, bush walks and good trout fishing in an unspoilt setting await the visitor, with launch trips, boats and fishing gear available from the lodge.

Lake Rotoiti Although there is a sprinkling of carved Maori meeting houses along its southern shoreline, activity on this elegant lake concentrates at Okere Falls township, near where Lake Rotoiti drains into the Kaituna River by way of an impressive waterfall. Its name, "little lake", refers to its larger neighbour, Rotorua, whose name in turn may be translated as "second lake". Roto itself means "lake".

Lake Rotorua The principal of the "hot lakes" group (so called for their surroundings rather than their temperatures), Lake Rotorua is roughly circular in shape, with alluring Mokoia Island almost in its centre. The city of Rotorua spreads along its southern perimeter. The lake has long been highly regarded by trout fishermen, and a number of trout springs around its edges display free-run trout of gargantuan proportions. In recent times the run-off of fertilisers from farmland that ultimately drains into the lake has brought a prolific growth of weed. This at one time threatened to "kill" the lake and its containment has taxed local and national ingenuity. Boats are for hire, and scenic trips run both on the lake (by boat) and over it (by float plane), all from the wharf on The Parade in Rotorua.

Mokoia Island Lake Rotorua's solitary island beckons with an almost irresistible call. Certainly so it proved to the maiden Hinemoa, whose home was near Rotorua at Hinemoa Point and who fell in love with Tutanekai, a warrior who lived on Mokoia. Hinemoa's family would not agree to the match, but eventually she swam to her lover through the night, guided by the sound of his plaintive flute.

TE WAIROA BURIED VILLAGE *Inundated in an eruption, it is still being uncovered.*

RONGO *A kumara god on Mokoia Island, placed with crops to assure a good harvest.*

KAINGAROA *Deep in the vast pine forest planted on the once-barren pumicelands.*

Ohinemutu A Maori village of considerable character by the lake and within Rotorua's city limits, Ohinemutu was the Maori settlement from which today's city was born. Uniquely it survives, with its splendid meeting house (some of whose carvings are reputed to be almost 200 years old), its quaint Tudor-styled church and, between the two, an odd ceramic bust of Queen Victoria. This was presented to the local Arawa tribe by her son, the Prince of Wales, in gratitude for the support given by the tribe to the colonial government during the Land Wars.

In fact, the support sprang simply and purely from traditional hostility felt towards some of the tribes committed to the wars, and siding with the government afforded the Arawa an excellent opportunity to settle some old scores.

Rotorua The city had its beginnings beside the Maori village of Ohinemutu at the end of the Land Wars, as tourists came to marvel at the thermal activity in the area. Soon, with the building of the grandiose Tudoresque bath house in the Government Gardens, the infant settlement took on the character of a spa town. For generations it remained very much a tourist town, until the 1960s saw it develop as the country's fastest-growing centre – in 1950 there were about 120 manufacturing and trade factories within eight kilometres of the city centre; 20 years later there were over 1,000. Today the massive earnings from tourism are icing on a more substantial industrial cake, and industry is taking a greater interest than hitherto in the potential afforded by thermal water, putting it to use in timber kilns, market-garden hothouses, mushroom farms and plant nurseries. Among a plethora of sights are trout springs and the Agrodome, displaying sheep and shearing.

Te Wairoa Buried Village Foretold by the appearance of a phantom canoe on the waters of Lake Tarawera, a colossal eruption of Mt Tarawera in 1886 (heard as far away as Christchurch) split the mountain in two and overwhelmed the village used by visitors to the fabled Pink and White Terraces nearby. These silica terraces drew admirers from all parts of the world, but they fell victim to the holocaust, as did the tohunga who warned of the impending tragedy. The village ruins have been excavated in part, and are open to the public.

LAKE OKAREKA *One of the smallest of the lakes in the "hot lakes" district.*

Thermal areas Each of the various thermal areas has a character uniquely its own: "Whaka", with its geysers and its Maori village; Tikitere, whose fury is unsurpassed; Waimangu, sullen and brooding and with the crater of what was the world's largest geyser; Waiotapu, with its colours and its curious Lady Knox Geyser, first brought to life by prisoners washing clothes with soap in a hot pool; Orakei Korako, with huge silica terraces hinting of what the volcano destroyed.

HONGI'S TRACK *Cutting a swathe through the bush on the Whakatane highway, the road follows a track used by Hongi Hika in 1823 as he brought men and canoes from Northland with which to lay siege to the Arawa tribe's stronghold on Mokoia Island.*

SWAN AND CYGNETS *A typical lake scene.*

KIWI AT RAINBOW SPRINGS *The timid and nocturnal kiwi is very rarely seen in the wild.*

Taupo

FABULOUS FISHING *The rivers and streams that feed Lake Taupo offer unsurpassed trout fishing.*

POWERFUL STEAM *Experience in power generation at Wairakei renders local engineers world leaders in geothermal technology.*

The vast waters of Lake Taupo extend over 650 square kilometres in the very heart of the North Island. Taupo township faces south, down the length of the lake to the distant, mauve tableau formed by the smoke and the snow of the peaks of Tongariro National Park. The lake bed, the depth of which remains unknown, was until comparatively recently the scene of frenzied activity: pumice flung in eruptions from its basin only 2,000 years ago deluged much of the central North Island and reached as far as Gisborne. Today the lake assumes a quiescent air, ruffled only by fishermen, boat owners and the occasional squall that necessitates constant vigilance on the water. The surrounding landscape is plainly mantled with pumice as witness to the past.

Thermal activity is much in evidence: at Wairakei, where steam feeds electric turbine generators and wafts high and wide across the countryside; at Tokaanu, and at Taupo itself, where there are public thermal baths and a number of fortunate private dwellings with their own hot pools.

1. *Celmisia, the mountain daisy, is after grass the most common plant on the New Zealand mountainside.* 2. *New-born lambs herald the arrival of spring. Until recently much of the area's potential pastureland would not, in the absence of cobalt, carry stock.* 3. *Tutu (Coriaria), one of the few poisonous species of native plant.* 4. *Trolling on Lake Taupo: the purist will always prefer casting a fly.*

"THE PICKET FENCE" *Patient anglers line the mouth of the Waitahanui River.*

SCOURGE OF THE FISHERMAN *Energetic holidaymakers prepare to water-ski on the lake.*

FORESTRY *Above*: Vast areas of pine forest are a feature of the countryside to the north, and huge timber trucks are commonplace. *Below*: The gigantic Kinleith pulp-and-paper mill rises from the farmland.

Kaingaroa State Forest What is reputed to be the world's largest man-made forest owes its existence to a depression (which gave rise to cheap labour) and the discovery of a cobalt deficiency in the pumicelands (which had rendered the plain "unavailable" for farming). Sprawling over some 150,000 hectares, it supplies vast quantities of logs to feed pulp-and-paper mills. Sawn logs are also shipped to Japan from Mount Maunganui.

Murupara The town developed after the 1939–45 war to capitalise on the maturing radiata pine of the Kaingaroa State Forest. The timber town rails logs to Kawerau's mill. There are some obscure Maori cave drawings in the forest nearby.

Opepe The site of a long-abandoned Maori village, this spot on the Napier Road about 17 kilometres from Taupo was where, in 1869, a detachment of troopers was ambushed. Five escaped, but the graves of the nine who died may be seen near the road (*follow the signposted track*). A short walk away is the old water-trough where the troopers had watered their horses while Te Kooti's scout watched, unobserved, from the bush.

Orakei Korako A spectacular series of multi-coloured silica terraces is the focal point of this thermal valley on the lip of the Waikato River north of Taupo. The steaming formations are reached by jet boat across the river. Just downstream is the Ohakuri hydro-electric dam.

Taupo Fishing, thermal pools, geo-thermal power, a vast lake, a fearsome waterfall and sensational rapids – Taupo has widespread appeal. Sited on the northern shores of the lake, where the mighty Waikato River is born, the town has a highly individual character, marked by rising steam and scrub-covered pumicelands. European settlement began in 1869 with the arrival of the Armed Constabulary, come to hound the enterprising Te Kooti. Their name survives at the thermal A.C. Baths, and the remains of their redoubt are, appropriately enough, near the police station. In addition to its service role, Taupo is a popular place to which to retire (and fish), and its population is in summer swollen with holidaymakers from all over the North Island. It is also favoured by travellers as a restful midway point on the trip between Auckland and Wellington on Highway 1.

Baked trout with cream
Truite Taupo

For those who are caught with a trout but are without a recipe book, and who wish to do more than simply fry it or poach it in rosé.

Butter, shallots, herbs, white wine, cream, lemon juice

Place trout to feed two persons on a buttered, shallow baking dish that has been sprinkled with 2 chopped shallots. Season with salt, pepper, a pinch of thyme and a bay leaf. Pour 4 tablespoons of melted butter over the trout and bake at 190°C for 25–35 mins, basting it several times with butter from the dish. Remove the trout carefully to a hot platter. Deglaze the pan with 3 tablespoons of white wine and ¼ cup of thick cream and strain the resulting sauce into a small saucepan. Boil it briefly to reduce the sauce a little and add salt and pepper (if needed) and a few drops of lemon juice. Pour sauce over the fish and serve at once.

HIGHWAY VIEW *Countryside north of Taupo, near Wairakei.*

TIMELESS TOKAANU *On the southern shore of the lake, at the foot of Pihanga, this settlement has much old-world charm and a lively history.*

LAKE VIEWS 1. *The lake's outlet, birthplace of New Zealand's longest river, the Waikato.* 2. *Acacia Bay, on the lake's northern shore.*

KAINGAROA FOREST *Highway 5 passes through radiata pine in the world's largest man-made forest.*

THE SCENE TO THE SOUTH *The summer view across the Desert Road (which runs south from Turangi to Waiouru) westwards to snowcapped Mt Ruapehu, a major winter ski resort.*

Lake Taupo The bed of the country's largest lake is technically a "caldera" – an enlarged volcanic crater formed by the collapse of the cone. The last eruption took place about 2,000 years ago, when vast areas were literally showered with pumice, and there are hot springs at various points around the lake shore – including some in the lake bed itself – relished by swimmers at Taupo township. With the land thought to be unsuited for farming, it was thermal activity which first attracted interest in the area. The trout for which the lake and its feeder streams and rivers are renowned were first introduced in 1890. Boats, rods and tackle may all be hired: there is no closed season for trout here, although fishing licences are required.

Tokaanu An endearing, enduring village, contrasting with the newness of neighbouring Turangi, Tokaanu rests at the southern end of the lake. Behind the settlement is one of the power stations for the Tongariro hydro-electric project. Although Tokaanu means "cold stone", there is a thermal area here, with open-air swimming baths, a small geyser and much belching mud. St Paul's Anglican Church, a memorial to the area's first missionary, displays a bell shattered by enthusiastic converts as they summoned local Maori to prayer.

Tokoroa By the edge of the Volcanic Plateau in the Upper Waikato basin is one of the country's fastest-growing centres. Tokoroa exploded from hamlet to city in only two decades as the huge pulp-and-paper complex at Kinleith became established.

Turangi Built as a hydro town for the Tongariro power scheme (whose information office is here), the town was designed to become the service centre for southern Taupo. Nearby, in the Tongariro River, is some of the world's finest trout fishing, and beside it a trout hatchery where rainbow trout are reared to stock the country's streams. Trout ova are also sent overseas.

Waihi A minute settlement charmingly sited by the water's edge not far from Tokaanu. The quaint church, decorated in Maori style, has stained-glass windows depicting both Christ and the Virgin as Maori. Near the church is the Te Heuheu mausoleum in which a number of the paramount chiefs of the Tuwharetoa tribe lie buried. Also close by is a comparatively recently carved meeting house which, in customary fashion, incorporates many venerable carvings previously housed in the succession of meeting houses that have stood on the same site over many generations.

1. Christ depicted as a Maori in the Catholic Church of St Werendfried at Waihi. 2. The interior of St Werendfried's, decorated in Maori style. The church dates from 1889. 3. Detail from the east window, with the Virgin Mary shown as Maori. 4. The bell at St Paul's, Tokaanu, shattered by over-enthusiastic bellringers and preserved as a testimonial to missionary endeavour.

PIHANGA SCENIC RESERVE *A segment of the bush skirts of soft, gentle Pihanga as she rises south of Lake Taupo. Her silhouette and mood lend themselves readily to the myth that tells of a battle between the neighbouring volcanoes for her favours. Her outline, however, disguises the fact that she, too, is of volcanic origin and so must be ranked as "male" as the rest of the group.*

KOWHAI *Honey-rich flowers of spring.*

HUKA FALLS *The Waikato River plunges.*

Wairakei Billowing steam and a deafening, though muffled, roar mark the scene of an imaginative scheme to tap thermal resources close to the surface and convert them into electricity. Innovations made here have passed into standard practice for this type of engineering, one increasingly resorted to in an energy-conscious era. Visitors are welcome at an information centre, where the technicalities are explained, and on conducted tours around the two power-houses. A

palatial hotel incorporates comfortable conference facilities and an excellent golf course. Nearby are the Huka Falls (where the full force of the Waikato bounds over an 11-metre ledge), Huka Village (an historical recreation) and the Aratiatia Rapids (almost a kilometre of foaming, lashing river which has been preserved, despite the Waikato's being diverted for power generation, and which is "turned on" from 2.30 p.m.–4 p.m. when circumstances permit).

LAKE ROTOAIRA *A bush-girt lake, 20 kilometres from Turangi, whose precincts are a special reserve of the Maori people.*

Tongariro National Park

TONGARIRO AND NGAURUHOE *An early Polynesian, Ngatoroirangi, is said to have climbed Ngauruhoe* (centre) *to claim the area for his followers. There, in the perishing cold, he prayed for warmth – and was rewarded with volcanic fire.*

RUAPEHU AND THE CHATEAU Less flamboyant than Ngauruhoe but an active volcano nonetheless, Ruapehu is the most popular peak in the North Island with winter sports enthusiasts. From time to time the waters of its crater lake have rewarded both skiers and climbers with the luxury of a warm swim on the very roof of the North Island, but renewed activity in recent years has seen the temperatures soar.

In a land of contrast and spectacle, none is more vivid than the snow-clad peaks of Tongariro National Park as they soar above the Rangipo Desert. No mountain could be more spectacular than the generally quiescent, lava-lined volcano of Ngauruhoe when in full-throated eruption.

The moods, the mists and the awesomeness of an area still witnessing creation conspire to lend magic to mythology. The peaks in eruption were portrayed as giants feuding for the love of Pihanga, a demure, bush-clad mound at the southern extremity of Lake Taupo. Yet another rival, the alluring Taranaki (Mt Egmont), was driven out, leaving the great gash of the Wanganui River as it flows westward to the sea and ensuring its perpetual isolation.

The park, given by the tribe upon trust for the purpose, preserves in perpetuity a region sacred to the Tuwharetoa.

KETETAHI SPRINGS *Hot springs on the slopes of Tongariro.*

POUTU CANAL *Part of the Tongariro power scheme.*

CREEPING *Myrsine nummularia.*

MOUNTAIN HEATH *Sub-alpine flora tints the plateau in late summer.*

WAIOURU ARMY MUSEUM *A nation's military history is commemorated.*

TAWHAI FALLS *Talk of a haunted whare here lends the falls a supernatural air.*

Whakapapa Activity centres in the main on Whakapapa village, where are found the Chateau (a government-owned hotel complete with golf course), the park headquarters and a well-equipped camping ground with cabins. Beyond lie the Whakapapa ski fields, the first on the mountain to be developed. In summer the headquarters organise conducted tramps and climbs of Ruapehu and Tongariro (there are also numerous marked tracks for independent walkers); in winter chairlifts from the top of the Bruce Road make for an easier ascent. From here, too, it is possible within one day to ski down a mountain, enjoy a thermal swim and catch a trout from either Lake Taupo or the Tongariro River – a more leisurely pace is recommended.

The weather on the mountain can change rapidly, and visitors are warned of the mountain's unpredictable character. Seismic activity is closely monitored, but Ruapehu has been known suddenly to eject vast quantities of hot water, mud and boulders.

Desert Road The name given to the bleak and barren road between Waiouru and Turangi. On a clear day the mountains' presence dominates, but in winter snow and ice force the motorist to eschew scenery and concentrate on the road.

Ohakune The development of the Turoa ski fields has turned a market-garden and timber town into a major winter resort.

Te Porere A tussock fort, built by Te Kooti in 1869, has been restored by the Historic Places Trust.

Waiouru A major Army camp uses much of the volcanic plateau for military exercises. The Queen Elizabeth II Army Memorial Museum traces the country's involvement in conflict.

TE HEU HEU TUKINO IV A bust of the paramount chief of the Tuwharetoa stands in the park headquarters. It was he who led the Taupo forces into battle against the Pakeha in the Waikato and who later supported Te Kooti. Alarmed at the prospect of his tribe's sacred mountains being used as trig stations, he succeeded in preserving their tapu by ceding them in 1887 to the people of New Zealand as the country's first national park.

ASPECTS OF RUAPEHU *The Pinnacles (above) and a ski lesson (below).*

OHAKUNE TOWNSHIP *The focus for recent development of Ruapehu's southern slopes, Ohakune is alive with activity in the winter months.*

Manufacturing industries

The manufacturing sector of the country's economy is very much the junior partner to agriculture, and is dominated by activities which either add value to agricultural goods (as in food processing and the manufacture of wood products) or which meet the specific needs of farmers (as in the assembling and servicing of vehicles).

From the outset New Zealand was cast in the role of supplier to Britain of "colonial products" – food, wool and raw materials – while remaining reliant on her for manufactured goods, investment and shipping. Before the age of steam, shipping costs afforded a high degree of protection for would-be manufacturers, whose ventures began as, for example, boot-making factories to supply the needs of gold miners or woollen mills to eliminate the need to import back from Britain yarn spun from New Zealand wool.

The importance of farming, too, fostered the early development of engineering skills, the blacksmith soon becoming a maker of ploughs and harrows and, eventually, of the sophisticated farm machinery which has led local technology to be in high demand around the world. The processing of farm products was also important after the introduction of refrigeration, when meat works and butter and cheese factories sprung up all around the country. Protective tariffs helped protect the home market for clothing and textiles, and they geographically sheltered others such as brickworks, breweries and the makers of bulky furniture and perishable goods.

The shortages induced by two world wars provided further stimulus for home production when huge quantities of goods were produced for the Armed Forces. Since then, and encouraged by a blend of tariffs, import licensing and export incentives, manufacturing has grown, both to substitute home products for imports and to process raw materials. Periodic collapses in world prices for grassland products, too, have heightened awareness of the country's narrow economic base and of its vulnerability in the face of unpredictable pricing trends. This has been further squeezed by Britain's entry into the EEC and New Zealand's subsequent denial to the very markets which brought its economy into existence. To make matters worse, markets carefully cultivated elsewhere have been upset by the EEC's dumping of surplus produce there. Also significant in fostering New Zealand manufacturing have been an increasingly urbanised population and a closer economic relationship with Australia.

The pressure is on New Zealand's manufacturers to perform as never before. In this they are handicapped by a small home market, where comparatively short production runs result in an expensive final product. However, the country has a cheap labour force compared with other market economies: OECD figures in 1983 showed the per capita GDP as less than that of the United Kingdom, about two-thirds that of Australia and just over half that of the United States.

NEW ZEALAND STEEL *The Glenbrook Steel Mill in South Auckland draws on Wai ironsand deposits for the production of a wide range of steel products. Projected expan of the works aims to see output raised to 770,000 tonnes a year from 1984.*

ALLIANCE FREEZING WORKS *The mutton chain at Southland's giant meat works (ir right).*

JET BOAT MANUFACTURE *A New Zealand "first" for Canterbury engineer-farmer, late Sir William Hamilton, led to exciting developments in the engineering field. The Hami jet unit is renowned the world over, with production based in Christchurch (inset far righ*

Taranaki

MOUNTAIN AND MILK *Mt Egmont viewed from Inglewood, with the inevitable and ubiquitous dairy herd in the foreground. Mt Egmont is often compared with Japan's Fujiyama.*

RICHMOND COTTAGE (1853) *An early New Plymouth home.*

The lone sentinel of Mt Egmont visually and climatically dominates a lush, verdant region. Her 2,518-metre peak sweeps symmetrically from a low coastal landscape to precipitate rain from moisture-laden westerly breezes: this falls on a lowland area floored with ash deposits from the dormant volcano. On this combination of blessings Taranaki's prolific dairy industry is based, with dairy cows in milk in some areas outnumbering sheep shorn by more than two to one. The cows themselves are among the country's most productive.

The discovery of vast fields of natural gas both on and offshore has given a new purpose to the region's development, with New Plymouth, its urban heart, at last reaping the benefits from hydrocarbons which for over a century had proved elusive. These finds have helped afford some modest cushioning to the country's economy in recent times, but their full exploitation has required an unprecedented level of investment, most of it in foreign currency. Much of this has been spent in the Taranaki region.

Egmont National Park The sacred mountain of the Taranaki was returned to the tribes in 1978 in a symbolic gesture, to enable them to give it voluntarily to the people of New Zealand. The peak's magic pervades a wide surrounding area; it served as a burial ground for chiefs and such was its tapu that guides would only accompany the first European climbers as far as the perpetual snowline, and then pray for their safe return. Three "mountain houses" serve as bases for visitors – Dawson Falls, Stratford Mountain House and the North Egmont Chalet. There is a variety of good walks and the climb to the summit is an easy one in good conditions.

OIL AND GAS New Plymouth was quickly in the oil stakes: the first find in the British Empire was made here in 1856, barely seven years after the world's first commercial strike had been made in the USA. With the advent of the motorcar came "Peak", the city's own brand of petrol which was refined here from local oil. Only one pump remains from the old field (*2, above*), in Bayly Road. In 1969 came a gas strike at Kapuni (*3, above*), from where gas is now piped to many parts of the North Island. This in turn was eclipsed by massive offshore finds (*1, left*). These require the skills perfected in Europe's North Sea to bring it ashore, and give the country so much gas that it has taken some years for decisions to be made on its exploitation.

CHEESE *Still a major cheddar producer, Eltham now makes many varieties – such as this blue vein cheese.*

SHOPPING IN STYLE *New Plymouth's Devon Street Mall, an indication of the region's growth and prosperity.*

MT EGMONT The isolation of Egmont from other mountains gives it a distinctive flora, but the mountain (viewed here from Dawson Falls) is in fact part of a chain of volcanic peaks which stretches to the Sugar Loaf Islands, offshore from New Plymouth. A sustained series of eruptions built the symmetrical cone. The myth explaining the mountain's solitude is recounted on p. 70

New Plymouth The country's "oil boom" city exploded into prominence with the discovery of vast fields of natural gas both on and off shore. These, and subsequent finds of oil, came when fuel costs were biting heavily into the highly mechanised farming industry and rapidly eroding returns from exports. Hitherto "Taranaki" had been synonymous with "cheese" and New Plymouth was the world's largest exporter of cheddar – a title lost when the EEC closed New Zealand's access to the British market.

Pukekura Park is one of the country's finest gardens, with neighbouring Brooklands Park affording an elegant setting for outdoor performances. A small lake in front of the stage mirrors the performers. Some 29 kilometres away is the 360-hectare Pukeiti Rhododendron Trust, nestling between the Kaitake and Pouakai Ranges. Duncan & Davies nursery (*Westown*) exports native plants all over the world. The museum (*cnr Brougham and King Streets*) and art gallery (*Queen Street*) house excellent collections. St Mary's Church (1842) (*Vivian Street*), backed by Cherry Blossom Walk and the lookout on Marsland Hill, is the oldest stone church in the country. Richmond

Cottage, by the museum, is one of the city's earliest buildings.

Hawera The principal town of South Taranaki boasts a spectacular dairy factory. The pre-European pa site at nearby Turuturumokai is also worth a visit.

Manaia The township centres on a war memorial while on its golf course stand two well-preserved blockhouses built by the Armed Constabulary during the Land Wars. To the north, at Kapuni, lie gasfields which feed the North Island grid.

Opunake A modest dairying centre where cheese for export was first produced in Taranaki. Nearby, at Oaonui, is the on-shore treatment station for gas from the Maui field. Condensate is extracted for refining at Whangarei before the gas is fed to Kapuni and into the North Island pipeline grid.

Waitara Scene of the outbreak of the Land Wars between Maori and Pakeha, the former Maori riverside stronghold has a huge freezing works. Nearby Motonui is the site of the world's first plant to produce petrol from natural gas using Mobil's advanced catalystic technology.

MANUKORIHI PA At Waitara stands a memorial to Sir Maui Pomare (1876–1930), a Maori leader who did much to restore the fortunes of his people after the Land Wars. It was at Waitara in 1860 that land tensions between Maori and settler erupted into war after the government used troops to enforce a patently defective transaction. Fighting engulfed much of the North Island and provided the pretext for further land confiscations. Pomare is likened to the legendary Maui (who fished the North Island from the ocean) as he "fished" compensation for the land from a sea of sorrow.

GAS-FIRED STATION *New Plymouth.*

IRONSAND At Waipipi, deposits are extracted from poor land, turned into a slurry and pumped out to tankers for shipment to Japan.

PUKEITI RHODODENDRON TRUST *Azaleas, rostas and, of course, rhododendrons abound.*

Wanganui and environs

A DEEP, GREEN, LIMPID RIVER *A gorge on the Wanganui River, just one of the series of elegant scenes that awaits the traveller.*

TE KOOTI'S BATTLE-FLAG *The wily rebel's flag now reposes in Wanganui's museum.*

VICTORIAN FACADES *Wanganui's Victoria Avenue.*

AT PEACE *River wildlife is little disturbed.*

The city of Wanganui exudes a mellow air, which derives both from its origins as one of the earliest of the New Zealand Company's settlements and its superb site near the mouth of the wide Wanganui River. Inland the river is narrower, flowing down from the volcanoes of the Tongariro National Park and winding through virgin bush and spectacular scenery before broadening to enter tidal reaches. In mythology the river's course was hewn by massive Mt Egmont as it retreated to safe ground, badly wounded, after losing a lovers' battle with the fiery Tongariro.

In pioneer times boats of settlers and Maori canoes shuttled to and fro, trading up and down the river, but the Wanganui is no longer the major waterway it once was, and the demise of coastal shipping has stilled a once-busy sea port. The city is now established, if not wholly secure, in the role of manufacturing centre, but it has suffered from its proximity to other centres now better served by transport.

Added character is lent the city by Putiki pa, a riverside Maori settlement within the city limits, which has a splendidly decorated church. The Maori treasures in the city museum, too, are among the finest of any provincial centre.

JERUSALEM *An agreeably named Catholic mission station, where an international nursing Order began, situated downriver from Pipiriki.*

MAKER AND MADE *Mt Egmont, viewed from near the Wanganui's source, is said to have gouged out the river bed on its journey west.*

CITY AND RIVER *Wanganui city, its suburbs and river viewed from Durie Hill's tower.*

RESTORED RIVERBOAT *Now a ferry for sightseers up and down the Wanganui River.*

Bulls The oddly titled junction town by the Rangitikei River has a name which honours an artist rather than its dairying activities. The carver James Bull established the hotel and store around which the town eventually formed after having done work on the British House of Commons at Westminster. Nearby are Flock House, an agricultural college whose graduates have made significant contributions to the country's agriculture, and the New Zealand Air Force base at Ohakea.

Marton A prospering farming town, with several nationally known schools, Marton was re-named for Captain Cook's birthplace more out of desperation than from any desire to honour the navigator who was never anywhere near here. Its shocked residents had discovered that its sonorous Maori name of Tutaenui actually meant "dung heap". Splendid homesteads abound, the finest being "Westoe" (1874), built by Sir William Fox, who was four times Premier but is today better remembered for his watercolours than for his political achievements. The town of Foxton is named for him.

Raetihi Originally built as a timber town, which has since broadened into sheep- and cattle-raising as well as some dairying and market gardening, Raetihi first developed on a level clearing where wagoners could overnight on the way to and from Pipiriki, the point on the Wanganui River that then served as the district's principal point of access.

Ratana The country's only religious settlement of substance was founded by followers of Wiremu Tahupotiki Ratana who, in 1918, here experienced the vision that was to change his own life and that of countless thousands. His vision led him to found the Ratana religion, and so kindle a revival of Maoridom that over 60 years later continues to blaze. The movement, initially conceived simply as a catalyst to draw Maoris into the estab-

lished Christian churches, developed into a Church in its own right. The Ratana Temple here is heavy with symbolism, and a museum (which can occasionally be visited) contains the crutches and other aids of invalids cured by Ratana, whose prowess as a faith-healer has few equals.

Wanganui The "River City" sprawls across the tidal reaches of the Wanganui River, a city with a feeling of substance that derives from its origins as one of the first New Zealand Company settlements. Queen's Park is its cultural centre, with a good small art gallery and a museum that has a particularly strong Maori collection. The suburb of Putiki, by the river, marks the site of the original Maori settlement and has a fine carved meeting house, an old *pataka* (storehouse) and a flamboyantly decor-

ated Maori church. At Cooks Gardens, Peter Snell in 1962 set the first of his world records for the mile, and on St John's Hill, surrounded by the gardens of the city's most exclusive suburb, is the showpiece of Virginia Lake. The best beaches are at Castlecliff (*8 kilometres*) and Kai-Iwi (*16 kilometres*).

Wanganui River Trips on the river range from the leisurely to the rapid, but to see the scenery to advantage it is necessary to venture up beyond Pipiriki. The river is navigable by small craft – from organised jet boats to canoes – for some 230 kilometres.

Waverley A farming centre close to the border with Taranaki, Waverley is known for curious Maori rock drawings (at Kohi) and the exploitation of coastal ironsands.

VIRGINIA LAKE *A tranquil city haven.*

PUTIKI CHURCH (1937) *One of the country's finest Maori churches.*

MEMORIAL LOOKOUT *On Durie Hill.*

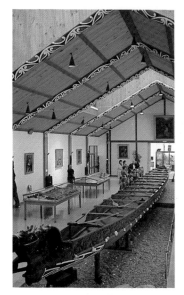

WAR CANOE *In the Wanganui Museum.*

RIVERSIDE SCENE *Tree ferns and waterfall.*

77

Manawatu

THE SQUARE *Te Awe Awe presides over Palmerston North's heart, with the Civic Centre in the distance.*

RANGITIKEI RIVER *Pictured near Ohingaiti, the river is noted for its fertile, intensively farmed terraces and steep-walled gorge.*

The Manawatu encompasses the largest plains to be found in the North Island, sweeping from the greywacke ranges of the Tararuas and Ruahines to lap the Tasman Sea. The ranges are cleaved by the imposing Manawatu Gorge, a cleft illogical in that here a river that rises on eastern slopes has turned about and cut its way through the range that gave it birth in order to reach the sea to the west. Elsewhere, by comparison with some other regions, the prospect appears to lack visual drama. However, closer acquaintance reveals the several rivers that formed the alluvial plains and a variety and intensity of farming activity that matches anything elsewhere.

Economically the region divides between dairying on the plains and fat-lamb production and the breeding of stud sheep on the downlands to the north-east. It focuses on Palmerston North, once a clearing in the bush, later a major rail junction, and now a city which ranks only behind Hamilton as the country's second largest inland metropolis. With Hamilton it shares international importance as a centre for agricultural research.

Manawatu's open, surf-swept beaches provide good fishing, but bathing in unpatrolled areas calls for caution. Rather, the region's opportunities for recreation lie inland, with fishing for trout in the rivers and tributaries or tramping in the foothills. The rivers also provide good settings for jet boating and for canoeing.

SUMMER NEAR MANGAWEKA *Dense forest has made way for peaceful pasturelands.*

TREE-LINED *Massey University's campus.*

OVER THE TOP *Palmerston's Civic Centre.*

FEILDING'S STOCKYARDS *Overseas as well as local buyers gather here for the Friday stock sales.*

HALL OF RUGBY FAME Appropriately sited in the capital of a rugby stronghold, the collection of ephemera engendered by the national passion grows steadily. 1. One of the immortal (1905 All Black) Billy Wallace's international rugby caps. 2. The coveted All Black jersey. 3. A rare French rugby poster. 4. The boot with which Geffin kicked five penalties in 1949 to deprive the All Blacks of a well-merited victory over South Africa.

Feilding The rich downlands around Feilding support many prized stud flocks and give the town a substance other farming centres close to major cities generally lack. Curiously, its layout is modelled on the English city of Manchester.

Hunterville A tiny sheep-farming centre whose spruce pastures were won from the bush, only fragments of which remain in Bruce Park and on Vinegar Hill.

Manawatu Gorge A grand canyon twisting through the ranges to link with Woodville and southern Hawke's Bay. Theories abound as to how the Manawatu managed apparently to defy the logic of geography in this extraordinary way. Perhaps the most likely explanation is that the ranges, which originally lay under the sea, sagged and then slowly rose out of the water so that the gap was gradually chiselled deeper to form a natural watercourse, to which the river adapted itself.

Palmerston North The city lies by the Manawatu River, close by the ranges that assure the region's rainfall. The bush that once clothed the plains has long fallen to the settler's axe, but abundant parks and a huge square are compensations. The city, in which education is the single most important industry, has long been at the forefront of agricultural training and research – Massey University has trained farmers for over 50 years, and comparatively recent expansion into other disciplines has helped give the city a vibrance it once lacked. The university, which includes the country's only veterinary school, has a research role but is dwarfed in this by the Grasslands Division of the Department of Scientific and Industrial Research, a seed-testing station, and both the Dairy Research Institute and the Dairy Board's artificial breeding centre at Awahuri. The city also boasts an impressive art gallery with an excellent contemporary collection. Museums include Totaranui (*Church Street*), the Hall of Rugby Fame (*Grey Street*) and a steam engine museum at Tokomaru.

Sanson A tiny junction settlement close by the Mount Lees Reserve, a rich and verdant setting in which to wander and to picnic amongst native and exotic plants.

Taihape There are some North Island towns marginally farther from the sea, but none with quite the same landlocked feeling. To the north of this once-railway town lies the wild Volcanic Plateau; to the east, the inland Patea route through the North Island's largest sheep runs to Hawke's Bay.

PLAIN PEDALLING *An easy mode of transport in a flat, unhurried city.*

TEACHER'S TRAINING *A marae and meeting house at the Palmerston North Teachers' College.*

"WATERFALLS" *A painting by New Zealand artist Colin McCahon which hangs in the Manawatu Art Gallery, Palmerston North.*

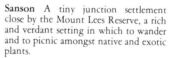

HISTORY PRESERVED *A vintage steam engine pictured at Feilding.*

MAIZE FIELD *Croplands near Marton.*

The Kapiti Coast and Horowhenua

THE CURL OF THE COAST *The shoreline and Kapiti Island viewed from the Paekakariki Hill. Kapiti served as the base for the warrior-chief Te Rauparaha, and as a shore whaling station.*

The curve of Tasman coastline arching north from Wellington enjoys a special place in the hearts of the capital city's inhabitants. An hour's drive (or less) from the heart of the city lies an unbroken stretch of grey sand beach, which not only provides year-round recreation but also enjoys a unique

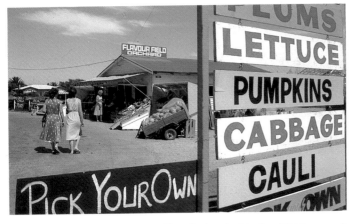

ROADSIDE BARGAINS *Fruit and vegetable stalls abound, with offers of "pick-your-own" a special temptation.*

micro-climate for commercial and private gardeners and the thousands of weekend "bach" owners who swell the Kapiti Coast's otherwise small permanent population. The several small seaside towns are a hive of weekend activity and together with those of the Horowhenua provide a focus for the rich market gardens and lush dairy farms which dominate the hinterland.

Wedge-shaped between the sea and the mountainous Tararuas and dissected by a number of rivers – the Waikanae, Ohau, Otaki and Manawatu – the alluvial coastal plain tapers from the broad expanses of Horowhenua to a bare roadwidth which, in the early days of Wellington, provided a natural defensive position. Its history is dominated by Te Rauparaha (c. 1768-1849), the Ngati Toa chief who, after being driven out of the Waikato, migrated to Kapiti Island where he traded with whalers and flax merchants for the guns he needed to ensure his domination not only of the immediate area but also of much of the South Island. His notoriety was a constant provocation to the Wellington settlers who, typical of their time, both misunderstood and undermined his personal *mana* and genuine attempts at reconciliation.

SOUTHWARD CAR MUSEUM *A unique museum complex situated at Otaihanga, between Paraparaumu and Waikanae, combines restaurant, conference and theatre facilities with a superb display hall containing over 120 vintage and classic cars dating back to 1895, as well as antique motor cycles, cycles, traction and fire engines. First opened to the public in 1979, it is one of the largest private collections in the world. Amongst the several exceptional exhibits is the Stutz Indianapolis racer (picture inset), one of only five ever made and thought to be one of only two still in existence.*

Foxton The town divides between the beach and the main road, reflecting its origin as a port and its life-blood since the port closed.

Kapiti Island Te Rauparaha's fortress is now largely a bird sanctuary, with a small area grazing sheep. It can occasionally be visited (permits are required). The surrounding seabed enjoys a high reputation with skin divers.

Levin The Horowhenua's principal centre, Levin is circled by prolific market gardens and is home to a variety of light industries. Lake Horowhenua is a pleasant picnic and boating spot, and Waitarere and Hokio beaches are also popular.

Otaki The oldest and most fascinating of the settlements, Otaki was. Te Rauparaha's mainland base and has long been populated. There is a small but interesting museum, an old Roman Catholic mission, a good beach and a comparatively new carved meeting house (a feature of the area generally is the number of small meeting houses seen from Highway 1). Pre-eminent is Rangiatea Church – built in 1849 and probably the finest of all the Maori churches. A drab exterior masks a breathtaking interior where full but considered reign is given to traditional Maori design. The ridge-pole is reputed to have been over 30 metres long before a local missionary, terrified that the building project would end in calamity, one night secretly sawed off about a tenth of its length. Opposite the church are memorials both to the Ngati Toa chief and to the coming of Christianity.

AKATARAWA VALLEY *The picturesque alternative route between Waikanae and the Hutt Valley and Wellington.*

Paekakariki, Paraparaumu and Waikanae A chain of seaside settlements faces out to Kapiti Island. With its rich soil, Waikanae is particularly favoured as a place to which to retire. Spectacular sunsets silhouette the distant South Island.

NETTING AT NIGHTFALL *One of the many groups who gather at Paekakariki Beach to net flounder.*

WAITARERE'S WRECK *The skeleton of the sailing ship* Hydrabad *has adorned the beach for over a century.*

Wairarapa

SUNRISE OVER THE WAIRARAPA COAST   *A generally wild stretch of coastline is broken here at Castlepoint.*

CENTREPOINT   *Masterton's modern mall.*

THE GOLDEN SHEARS The world's leading shearers gather in Masterton every March to pit their skills against each other in the country's premier shearing competition.

The well-groomed, prosperous Wairarapa Valley thrusts southward from Hawke's Bay to meet the sea prematurely in the broad but shallow Lake Wairarapa. The lake in turn drains into the smaller Lake Onoke, separated from the pounding Pacific Ocean by no more than a bar of shingle. To the west rises the bush-draped Tararua Range; to the east rolls hill country which drops, often precipitously, to the sea.

The lower valley was a grassy open plain that readily lent itself to sheep: the country's first pastoral farming took place here, on the eastern shores of Lake Wairarapa. Further north, however, the land was locked in forest and the familiar struggle was joined between hopeful, ill-prepared migrants and a relentless, unyielding terrain. Today's trim pasturelands and orchards are legacies of considerable struggle and heartbreak.

HOMEWARD   *A herd of milking cows makes its twice-daily trek to the milking shed.*

STRONG-HEARTED AND TOUGH   *A restored traction engine near Carterton.*

SHEEP COUNTRY *A typical Wairarapa landscape.*

Carterton Set in wide plains and graced with substantial market gardens and orchards, Carterton began as a bush settlement, and today's open spaces were wrested from the forest with considerable hardship. To the west rise the Tararuas, in which the Tararua Forest Park and its Mt Holdsworth Reserve and Waiohine River Gorge are particularly appealing spots. The Tararua Range as a whole is much used by trampers, both local and from Wellington.

Castlepoint A rare beach settlement on an otherwise generally bleak and wild stretch of coast, Castlepoint was named for a bastion-like rock, not for its fortress-like lighthouse. Beneath the light is a huge sea cave where a giant octopus is said to have hidden in a vain attempt to escape from the Polynesian explorer, Kupe, before it was chased around Cape Palliser and out into Cook Strait. The Maori used legendary tales to detail geography, and the tale served as an oral map to the region. The settlement is periodically the setting for entertaining picnic beach races.

PREPARING FOR THE STARTER *Castlepoint's annual beach races attract a festive crowd, who picnic and punt modestly on an equaliser which lets you know your horse only after you've placed your bet.*

Eketahuna On perhaps the prettiest site of all the Wairarapa townships, Eketahuna sits above the gorges of the Makakahi River.

Featherston Featherston nestles beneath the Rimutakas which divide the Wairarapa from the Hutt Valley. Nearby is the sweeping expanse of Lake Wairarapa. A sign on the Rimutaka Hill road reads simply: Beware of Wind.

Greytown Picturesque Greytown, an orcharding and market-gardening town, rests on rich river loam.

Martinborough A farming centre, whose main streets are in the shape of the Union Jack.

Masterton The hub of the Wairarapa reflects the affluence of the region and houses increasing industry. The generous grounds of Queen Elizabeth Park incorporate a boating lake and a memorial recording the traditional friendship between Maori and Pakeha in the region. The vigorous Wairarapa Arts Centre (Bruce Street) and the Mt Bruce National Wildlife Centre (24 kilometres north) are worth visits.

Pahiatua The centre for the upper Wairarapa has a broad street set aside by planners for the railway but never used by it.

Riversdale A sandy surf beach with swimming, fishing and a growing number of holiday baches.

NATIONAL WILDLIFE CENTRE Efforts to save the takahe *(pictured)* and other rare species are made at the National Wildlife Centre on the slopes of Mt Bruce, 24 km north of Masterton.

A WAIRARAPA BACH *Clusters of holiday cottages huddle wherever by-laws allow.*

FEATHERSTON'S FELL ENGINE Before a tunnel was driven through the Rimutakas, these nuggety little engines, with horizontal wheels to grip onto the sides of the rails, were used to haul trains over the range to and from Upper Hutt. Added to the steep grade was the furious wind, which once actually blew a passenger train from the tracks.

TARARUA BUSH *The Mt Holdsworth Reserve.*

The Hutt Valley

A DAY AT THE RACES *Trentham's racecourse is a focal point for Wellington's sporting (and social) life, as is the nearby Heretaunga Golf Club.*

The broad expanse of the Hutt Valley has absorbed much of the capital city's expansion of the past thirty years. Once devoted to market gardens and dairy farms, its rich soil now sprouts two cities – Lower Hutt, very much the larger, and Upper Hutt, farther up the valley – and a bewildering variety of industry. The seafront village of Petone might well have become the nation's capital had not the river's flooding forced the first settlers to move to Wellington.

VIEWS FROM THE HILL *The Hutt River lazily reaches Wellington Harbour.*

VIEWS FROM THE HILL *Overlooking Petone, oldest of the settled areas on the harbour.*

THE HUTT RIVER *The upper reaches, north of Upper Hutt, are popular with fly-fishermen.*

Eastern Bays Historically it was to the warmth of Eastbourne and Days Bay that Victorian and Edwardian gentlemen would move from Wellington for the summer's sun. Today the bays are commuter hamlets, crowded on sunny weekends. "Gentlemen" seek sun further afield.

Lower Hutt Bounded by sharply rising hills to west and east, the city spreads right across the valley floor and, on land reclaimed for industry, southwards out on to the old harbour bed. It houses a number of industries of national importance. Pre-eminent are major units of the Department of Scientific and Industrial Research, among them the Soil Bureau, the Dominion Laboratory, the Geological Survey and the Institute of Nuclear Sciences.

Petone Still with very much of a village atmosphere, despite its urban surroundings, Petone's spirit is traditionally demonstrated on the rugby field, where its club team has defeated all comers. On the foreshore landed Wellington's settlers from the "first four ships", an event recorded in a museum in the waterfront Provincial Memorial.

EASTERN BAYS *To swim, to sail, to laze. . .*

Upper Hutt A newly created city, Upper Hutt seeks an identity independent of its much larger neighbour. The yearling sales at Trentham racecourse attract international interest.

Wainuiomata A dormitory suburb for Wellington and the Hutt Valley. Its commuters enjoy magnificent views.

DOWSE GALLERY *"It's an illusion" exhibition in Lower Hutt.*

TUTIKIWI ORCHID AND FERN HOUSE This attractive building, in Myrtle Street, Lower Hutt, was designed to house the outstanding orchid collection of horticulturalist Herbert Poole and ferns from the Jubilee Park Fernery.

TUI *After the kiwi, perhaps New Zealand's most loved bird.*

EASTBOURNE *A colonial terrace house finds new life.*

LOWER HUTT *Flowers in the city's centre.*

Three views from Wainuiomata Hill. Pictured left and right are three segments of the magnificent panorama which presents itself on the road from Lower Hutt to Wainuiomata. On the extreme left is the industrial area of Gracefield, with Somes Island and Wellington beyond; progressively, the pictures pan to the Western Hills. This steep-faced range and the line of the Hutt River mark the Wellington Fault, a major fracture in the earth's crust that follows the line of the Southern Alps through Wellington and up the Hutt Valley to continue along the length of the main North Island mountain chain. The fault, which sweeps through Wellington city and follows the curve of the Hutt Road round the harbour before turning up the valley, is even more pronounced from the air.

VIEWS FROM THE HILL *Looking towards Lower Hutt city and the Western Hills.*

PIONEERS' LANDING-PLACE *Petone.*

Political life

New Zealand's political life turns on its capital, Wellington. Through its airport a steady stream of parliamentarians, commuting between their constituencies and the centre of government, is joined by representatives of myriad pressure groups journeying either to press a case for governmental action or to make representations to the unceasing round of committees as special interests are consulted on aspects of proposed legislation.

Although modelled closely on the Westminster style of government, there is now only a single House of Representatives, the Upper House (the Legislative Council) having been voted out of existence in 1950. Like Britain, there is no "written constitution", the relevant provisions being scattered through a number of Acts of Parliament, some of which are "entrenched" (such as the term of Parliament) so as to render their amendment in effect impossible in the face of significant opposition. However, the combined absence of a written constitution and of an Upper House has led to calls for constraints on a process that has come to be so dominated by the system of party "whips" that it is now a rarity for a Government Member even to abstain, let alone to vote with the Opposition. Curiously, the same loyalty has not been shown where it is, by convention, required. Members of Cabinet, the Ministers who in theory "advise" the Crown in the exercise of executive powers, must support Cabinet decisions collectively – no matter that they may have argued against them – or else resign. In recent years few Ministers have done either.

Parliament has a maximum life of only three years, the shortest of any democracy. Though some see this as too brief an interval for coherent policies to be pursued, when offered the option of a four-year term in a referendum in 1967, the voters rejected it overwhelmingly.

The titular Head of State is the Queen of England, as she is in about 15 other Commonwealth countries, with the Governor-General (appointed by her on the advice of the Prime Minister) acting in her general absence. The Head of Government is the Prime Minister, the leader of the block supported by the majority of the Members of the House of Representatives. There are some 95 of these, four of whom are Maori Members elected by those Maori who choose to enrol on the Maori (as opposed to the General) voters' roll. Because in recent years increasing numbers of Maori have been elected to represent general constituencies, the same need for the seats to ensure representation by Maori no longer exists, although there is an argument in favour of their retention. The general constituencies are so overwhelmingly Pakeha in composition that it would be difficult for their Members, who might happen also to be Maori, to advance a consistently Maori viewpoint.

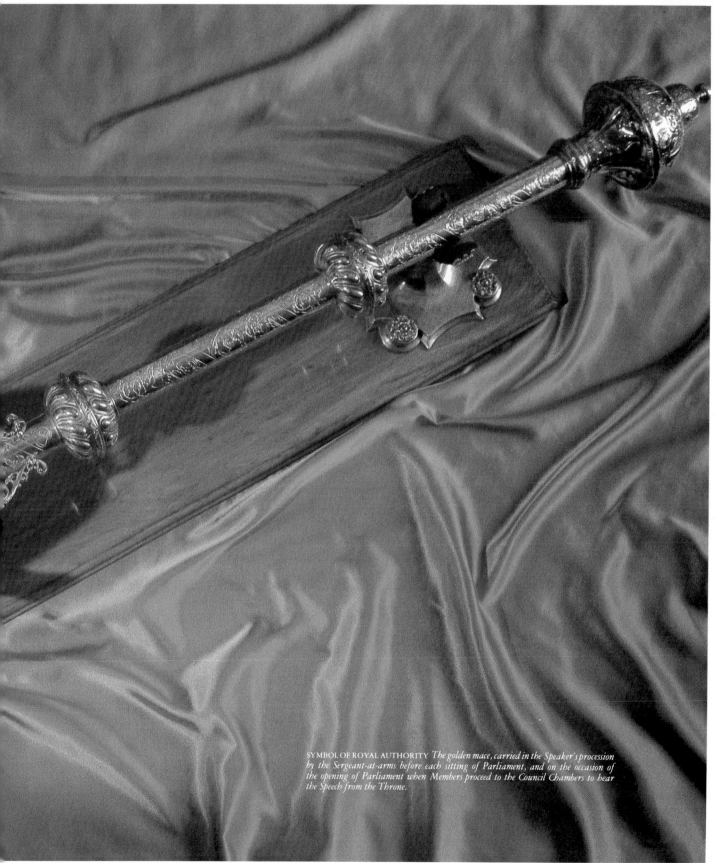

SYMBOL OF ROYAL AUTHORITY *The golden mace, carried in the Speaker's procession by the Sergeant-at-arms before each sitting of Parliament, and on the occasion of the opening of Parliament when Members proceed to the Council Chambers to hear the Speech from the Throne.*

Wellington

PARLIAMENT'S BEEHIVE *The statue of "King Dick" Seddon is in the foreground.*

MEANDERING LAMBTON QUAY *The street records in name and configuration the original shoreline, before reclamation began.*

Its houses sprinkled on the steep green slopes which skirt a splendid natural harbour, Wellington enjoys an incomparable setting of ever-changing mood. The beauty of the city on a clear, still day lingers in the memory and suggests that such days are of great frequency. Unfortunately boisterous winds well earn it the epithet "Windy Wellington", a reminder that the city is in the "roaring forties" and on the only break in a chain of mountains over 1,400 kilometres in length. The downtown area is largely reclaimed, somewhat discordantly, from the harbour, a process that has been continuing for over a century as a shortage of flat land bedevilled the settlement from the outset. To compound the problems of constructing high-rise buildings on reclaimed land is the fact that a major earthquake fault runs right through the commercial area, necessitating special design to accommodate the occasional tremors.

ALEXANDER TURNBULL'S HOME A wealthy bibliophile's home in Bowen Street is now a gallery and restaurant.

RISING HIGH *Economics dictate the balance between further reclamation and buildings rising higher. Of all New Zealand's cities, Wellington has the most spectacular skyline.*

HOME GROUND *The New Zealand Symphony Orchestra, based in Wellington, tours the country and beyond.*

EARLY MORNING AT EVANS BAY *A still dawn too frequently heralds a breezy day and tricky sailing for the yachts. On fine days these freckle the harbour, risking an upsetting from a sudden squall.*

The Maori likened the North Island to a fish – "the great fish of Maui" – and depicted its emergence from the sea as the "catch" of that great Polynesian hero. With its tail extending along Northland to Cape Reinga and with Taranaki and Hawke's Bay as its fins, the "great fish" has its head at Wellington. The country's capital rests on its nostrils.

The Wellington Peninsula is traversed by a number of faults, all recently active, several of them continuations of the fault lines that cross Cook Strait from Marlborough. The sharply rising hills dictate the city's layout and hamper communications with the northern hinterland. A solitary main road threads along the harbour shore out of the city, branching at Ngauranga to commence Highway One's journey north, and continuing around the harbour to the Hutt Valley.

Cook Strait, the only cleavage in a series of mountains that stretches from the southernmost South Island to East Cape, acts as a funnel through which a concentrated flow of air is forced, earning for Wellington its reputation for windiness. Gales of up to 100 km/h are experienced on about 30 days each year, most frequently in summer and in spring.

A QUIET FISHING SPOT *Evans Bay wharf.*

CUBA MALL *Setting for a water-mobile.*

RUGBY UNION'S HEADQUARTERS *Athletic Park, scene of epic encounters, is the national sport's home.*

KELBURN'S CABLE CAR *Much loved by commuters and sightseers alike.*

PARLIAMENT High Court judges in full-bottomed wigs parade for the formal opening of Parliament. New Zealand's legislature lacks an Upper House but – from its unwritten constitution and its procedures to the naming of the Members' restaurant – it is closely modelled on "the Mother of Parliaments" at Westminster.

TRADE FAIR *Newtown's Show Buildings.*

LADY NORWOOD ROSE GARDENS *A short walk from the city's centre and adjoining the Botanic Gardens, a profusion of colour and smells awaits the visitor.*

Even from 21,000 kilometres away, in London, it was apparent that Wellington, sited in the geographical centre of the country, was the logical place for the capital city. It was thus a priority for the New Zealand Company, under its "Wakefield Scheme", to establish a settlement here. Even before the Treaty of Waitangi was signed in February 1840, the first shiploads of migrants had arrived to establish themselves on the harbour shore at Petone. The Governor, though, had other plans, and there was a stormy relationship between these pioneers and the Auckland-based administration until, 25 years later, the seat of government was moved south. However, this was less the product of logic than the result of pressure from gold-rich Otago and a booming Dunedin, whose inhabitants could not accept a situation in which their only form of communication with the (much smaller) capital in Auckland was by way of Sydney. Even then the location was decided not by envious competing provinces but by a delegation

appointed by the Australian State Governors! The move has now effectively reversed the situation: Otago's gold dwindled and today it is Auckland that resents being governed from Wellington, with Dunedin as remote as ever.

The new settlers were fortunate to find that the winds which so battered their first makeshift homes had deterred substantial Maori settlement on the harbour. The Hutt Valley, too, was lightly peopled with the main concentrations of Maori population on the warmer and more hospitable coastal plains to the north. These lands were dominated by the "Maori Napoleon", the chief Te Rauparaha, from his base on Kapiti Island at the northern entrance to Cook Strait.

Although there were some skirmishes in the Hutt Valley, and the presence of the Ngati Toa war chief on Kapiti and at Paremata was unsettling, most local chiefs were willing to sell land, and the region was largely spared the conflict between Maori and Pakeha that so marred the early history of much of the North Island. The settlers were alarmed when Te Rauparaha was involved in an ugly incident in Marlborough in 1843, when an armed party of Nelson settlers misguidedly and illegally attempted to imprison him. He had signed the Treaty of Waitangi but did not regard this as offering an open door to European immigration. Later, after the aging chief had retired to Otaki and professed belief in Christianity, the newly arrived Governor, Sir George Grey, felt unsure of Te Rauparaha's intentions, and in July 1846 used troops to abduct him to Auckland, where he was held without charge until 1848.

A combination of political importance and a sheltered anchorage assured Wellington's steady growth over the years, though in more recent times the burgeoning of Auckland had taken its toll. With most of the country's population now living north of Lake Taupo, more and more head offices have moved north, and the region's relative importance as a manufacturing centre has similarly declined. As the seat of government, Wellington is home for the head offices

TOWARDS RED ROCKS *On the wild south Wellington coastline, a good walk from Owhiro Bay leads to both a seal colony and a curious upthrust of reddish volcanic rock.*

WOODEN COLOSSUS *"Government Buildings" (1876) is the world's second-largest timber building.*

LYALL BAY *A highly rated surf beach where even in the winter surfers brave the waves in wet-suits.*

COAT OF ARMS New Zealand's arms atop the wooden Government Buildings.

of international organisations and for representatives of foreign and Commonwealth governments. Based here, too, are numerous scientific, cultural and agricultural bodies.

Like no other New Zealand city, Wellington is a jumble of Victorian wooden buildings and modern high-rise office blocks, a mixture of colonial and computer eras. The houses perch at times precariously on the steep harbour wall, while the small apron of level land by the water is crowded with ever-taller commercial buildings. Parliament Buildings (*cnr Lambton Quay and Molesworth Street*), built in 1922 of grey Takaka marble from across Cook Strait, reflect the same contradictions, bridging the effervescent Gothic of its library wing (1897) with

the recently completed "Beehive" (1980). Arguments surrounding the building of the Library wing culminated in Prime Minister Seddon summarily ordering that the third storey be left off to save money. In fury, the architect had his own name removed from the foundation stone which, almost a century later, echoes his mute protest at the decision to "spoil the Architectural appearance of the edifice".

The site goes back to the settlement's origins, when it served as the home for the leaders of the New Zealand Company settlement. (Guided tours of the building provide a glimpse of the working of a Westminster-style of government, and it is possible to attend debates. The debates have been broadcast continuously since 1936, when the first Labour Government introduced the innovation as a way of countering what it saw as biased newspaper reporting.)

Behind Parliament Buildings stand more modern appurtenances of government, which in turn adjoin an historic pocket of Old Thorndon where quaint cottages in delightful disarray line pedestrian paths. Nearby, in Mulgrave Street, is Old St Paul's, a "Selwyn" church

which for a century served Wellington's spiritual needs and is now a tranquil setting for drama and concerts.

Lambton Quay, which has been progressively modernised over the last decade and is now a maze of hidden shopping malls and arcades, marks the original beachfront before reclamation pushed back the sea.

To the south of Lambton Quay sprawls the expanse of Government Buildings. Built of kauri and the second-largest wooden building in the world, it continues to house government departments more than a century after it was accorded a very quiet opening ceremony for fear of drawing attention to the fact that it had run wildly over its budgeted cost. Turnbull House *(Bowen St)*, once the home of bibliophile Alexander Turnbull, is used by community groups. The Alexander Turnbull Library itself, the core of which Turnbull bequeathed to the nation, is to be housed in the National Library. The Library's collections of Pacific material

and of Milton's works are world-renowned. Some distance away is the National Museum and Art Gallery *(Buckle Street)*. Special amongst its wild range of collections is a botany section dating back to specimens gathered by Cook's naturalists and others collected by the missionary-botanist Colenso. Included in excellent holdings of Maori material is the carved meeting house Te Hau-ki-Turanga (c. 1842). The finest surviving example of its kind, it was purchased from a Poverty Bay tribe in the euphoria of goodwill that followed the waiver in 1867 of some arbitrary confiscations of land in their area.

Across the Basin Reserve from the Museum lies the official residence of the Governor-General, the Queen's representative in New Zealand. New Zealand is one of more than a dozen independent countries which recognise the Queen of England as their formal Head of State.

The capital's architecture is a jumble of old and new, with highly organised pressure groups battling commercial interests (and occasionally the government) to preserve pockets of the city's colonial heritage. Particularly in Thorndon, old wood continues to defy modern concrete.

INNER-CITY RESIDENCES *Sydney Street, Thorndon.*

CONTRASTS *Plimmer House (c. 1872), Boulcott Street.*

OLD ST PAUL'S CATHEDRAL (1866) *Mulgrave Street.*

A HEAVILY STYLISED OPERA HOUSE *The New Zealand Opera Company performs Puccini's*
La Bohème *at the Wellington Opera House.*

ECHOES OF THE PAST *The Village shopping complex, Willis Street.*

PIGEON PARK *Courtenay Place affords a lunchtime resting place.*

Marine Drive Wellington's harbour is
sprinkled with rocky coves rather than
sweeps of sandy beach, but as compensation there is a magnificent marine drive
of some 40 kilometres, which can be extended to 90 kilometres by including the
run out around the harbour to Eastbourne. Start at Oriental Bay (a popular
lunchtime spot with office workers) and
drive with the sea on the left to skirt
Miramar Peninsula until finally Island
Bay and Owhiro Bay are reached. Return
by way of Happy Valley Road. The drive
passes Wellington airport.

Viewpoints The city is one of hills and
vantage points. Of the many, the pick are
Mt Victoria (which offers a sweeping
panorama and whose Maori name indicates that they, too, used it as a lookout)
and Tinakori Hill (festooned with wireless masts and affording an even more
sensational view). From Lambton Quay
the famous cable-car lifts pedestrians to

Kelburn and a pleasant corner of the
Botanic Gardens from which to savour
both the city and the harbour. Rather
than return to the city the same way, one
may walk down through the Gardens and
emerge a little distance from Parliament
Buildings.

Some beaches The pick of the city's
inner harbour beaches are Oriental, Worser and Scorching Bays; of the ocean
beaches, Lyall and Island Bays are well-suited for surfing. More distant beaches
to entice Wellingtonians are sun-drenched Eastbourne and Days Bay
across the harbour, and the endless tract
of sand up the Kapiti Coast, visited by
thousands each summer weekend.

MANSFIELD MEMORIAL New Zealand's most famous writer, Katherine Mansfield (1888–1923), is
inadequately remembered in
Murphy Street, but she herself
could scarcely wait to leave her
homeland, reflecting the negative view of New Zealand culture
that has mellowed only in relatively recent times. Wellington
she wrote, was "Philistia itself".
Yet curiously her most enduring
short stories all have a Wellington setting: "Prelude" (set in
Karori), "The Garden Party" (at
25 Tinakori Road) and "At the
Bay" (Days Bay). In Europe,
Katherine Mansfield was closely
associated with Virginia Woolf,
D. H. Lawrence and other literary
giants of the day. However "the
one peacock in our literary garden" in no way interpreted her
country to its people.

BASIN RESERVE *New Zealand cricketers engage India in a memorable test match. The area was "reserved" for use as an inner harbour
but was raised by the 1855 earthquake.*

THE SCENE AT MAKARA *In the distance is Mana Island, birthplace of the sheep industry, where 102 Merinos were landed in 1834 and from where the first wool was exported the following year.*

Hutt Valley Wellington's harbour fills a sea-drowned rivermouth, carved by the Hutt River along the line of the Wellington Fault. The valley, which provided the first extension of a land-starved city, has now blossomed into the cities of Lower and Upper Hutt.

Kapiti Coast A chain of sunny beaches and warmer settlements within comfortable commuting distance of the capital.

Makara A shingle beach on a wild stretch of coast with good fishing and diving is reached beyond the suburb of Karori. Makara Radio is the country's major receiving station.

Paremata An attractive seaside township, with the remains of a fort (1847) built to protect Wellington from the menace of Te Rauparaha's belligerent nephew Te Rangihaeata. His pa was by

pretty Pauatahanui Inlet (where a host of yachts now ride) on the site occupied by the tiny church of St Albans.

Plimmerton A pleasant commuter settlement. On its beach Te Rauparaha was kidnapped by British troops at dawn.

Porirua A much-maligned city, the

product of inept post-war planning, but one assuming its own special multi-cultural character.

Somes Island The larger of the harbour's islands seems to beckon but is in fact a quarantine station for imported animals. Its shore is less hospitable than distance suggests.

VIEW FROM NORTHLAND *Long overlooked by home buyers, the suburb has a sunny aspect.*

SURF LIFESAVERS AT LYALL BAY *The country's ocean beaches should be treated with respect.*